Contents

Foreword

This book is to some extent a re-write and a development of an earlier book of mine *Theory into Practice* published in 1997 which is now out of print. This earlier book, which concentrated on outdoor leadership, was criticised by some at the time (and rightly so) that despite its title it did not really give an indication of how to apply the theory discussed. In addition to focusing on leadership with young people this re-write is intended to address this issue in a more satisfactory manner. Significantly this book is more than twice the length of its predecessor, which gives me some hope that I have achieved something useful. The emphasis of the book remains, however, on translating the theory of leadership into practical usage. I have tried to avoid all the tricks that academics love; there are no big words or convoluted sentences (I hope!) and all the theory has been reduced to the basic understandable level. I know that some people will find fault with this or say that some areas have been oversimplified whilst others needed more emphasis: but I wanted to produce something that was both readable and useful; it would have been very easy to write a book of twice this length again. To this end the book does draw widely on the work of other people and a number of key texts in the fields of leadership and young people are extensively quoted. There are also a number of more direct contributions made by specialised writers in their own areas. Finally young people are directly quoted to give them a voice in how leadership is received. Any contentious statements are, of course, my own responsibility.

On a personal note I have been involved in leadership, of one sort or another, with young people for some twenty years now and it has to be said that I wish a book such as this had been available to me when I started out. My work with young people has been wonderful at times and hell at times. There have been magic moments and times when I wondered what was the point of it all. There have been times when I have been so proud of the young people that I have worked with and times when I have wanted to physically shake a bit of motivation into them. When I started out no one actually pointed out that the good times were really good and they had to be treasured and savoured because they were what gave it all meaning. Neither did anyone suggest that I got involved in understanding why and what I was doing. If this book can make life a little bit easier and a little bit more productive for anyone who leads young people, in whatever capacity, then its writing has been worthwhile.

Acknowledgements

I need to thank everyone who has contributed to the book, Di Collins, Phil Woodyer, Abi Paterson, Mick Wood and Judy Ling Wong as well as the young people who's quotes appear in the text and the people at Russell House Publishing for their support. Most of all I have to thank my partner, Sue, for her help and apologise for spending the whole of our valuable summer holiday stuck up in my study in front of a word processor. Sorry for being so obstreperous, I'm glad we've survived another book.

Introduction

Who This Book is For

The book is designed for a broad audience and although it may be partially true to say that if you work with young people this book is for you this would also be too glib an answer. This book is aimed at all those people, volunteer and professional, who work with young people outside of the 'mainstream', e.g. school and the educational system. This could mean youth workers, outdoor instructors and tutors, countryside rangers, community workers, scout leaders, Duke of Edinburgh's Award leaders and so on. In all of these fields there is no overt means of coercion: the leader leads through their leadership ability alone and not from a position of authority. That is not to say that these leaders are not in positions of great responsibility, or that teachers don't need leadership skills, but ultimately whether the young people in our care follow our lead is down to the way we work and the people we are. The use of theory and associated referencing should also make this a valuable book for students at all levels studying in the field of leadership with young people.

This book will not make you a great leader, what it will do is introduce some of the more relevant leadership theory and give you some idea of how to put it into practice. It will then be down to you to develop this through experience, reflection, learning from others and learning from mistakes; yours and others. In summary this book is about how the individual, you, interacts as a leader with young people, other books worth reading to give you a broader overview of working with young people include:

- Factor, Chauhan and Pitts (2001). *The RHP Companion to Working with Young People.*
- Wheal (1998). *Adolescence: Positive Approaches for Working with Young People.*
- Cooper (1998). *Outdoors with Young People.*
- Young (1999). *The Art of Youth Work.*
- Ogilvie (1993). *Leading and Managing Groups in the Outdoors.*

Using the Book

It was never intended that you should read through this book from cover to cover: although you are welcome to do so. Rather it is suggested that you use it as a 'dip-in' resource as and when you feel the need. The chapters do follow a fairly logical sequence but each one can be read by itself and still make sense. There are a few chapters that could be considered core reading which are worth dipping into first: Chapter 1 'Understanding Young People' discusses how young people are perceived by others and themselves and what this means to a leader working with them. Chapter 2 'Vision and Styles' goes to the heart of leadership and considers why and how leadership is used whilst Chapter 3 'Leadership Orientation' looks at the focus of leadership when working with young people. Of the others, Chapter 12 'Looking After Yourself and Others' and Chapter 14 'Rules, Roles and Responsibilities' are worth reading sooner rather than later as they might just save you a lot of grief at a later stage.

There are a number of suggested activities as part of appropriate chapters. These however, can be nothing more than an introduction to a broader area. The same is also true of many of the subjects covered in this book and the texts mentioned above are worthy of investigation.

Introducing Leadership

There are many theories as to why people become leaders and what makes great leaders. The longest running of all these arguments is whether leaders are born or made. Bass (1989) suggests that leadership potential in people is developed for one of three reasons:

1. Some trait in their character or personality means that they will naturally adopt leadership roles. This is usually referred to as 'trait' theory.

2. A crisis or similar event causes a person to 'rise to the occasion' and demonstrate extraordinary leadership abilities. This is sometimes referred to as the 'great events' or 'contingency' theory.

3. People choose to become a leader and adapt leadership roles through learning and experience. This is sometimes referred to as 'transformational leadership' theory.

It is probably nearer the truth to say that many of us come to positions of leadership through a combination of all three reasons. This book considers why people become leaders and suggests that people themselves question why they are leaders. However, its main purpose is to discuss more of what leaders do and how to be leaders as well as, more importantly, how to be effective leaders.

It is probably worthwhile before going any further to explore what do we mean by leadership and to ask how is this different from simply working with young people. Graham (1997: pp11–12) remarks that:

> *Leadership is not a science to be picked up in one book or course, but an art to be learned over time. It's not simply a set of rules to be followed, but an ability to build relationships. It's not merely skills and techniques, but a subjective blend of personality and style. Leadership involves not only the body and the mind, but the spirit and character as well: good leaders have the intuition, compassion, common sense and courage it takes to stand and lead.*

This seems a lot to ask of any one person and it is certainly true that some of the dimensions of leadership that Graham highlights could be considered innate whilst others might be learnt. This should not, however, preclude you from thinking of yourself as a leader of young people. Everyone has their own unique skills and leadership styles (see Chapter 2 Vision and Styles). Leadership is not a fixed skill; it varies from person to person. No one can be sure until they try it how they will react to the challenge which leadership imposes. What we can be sure about is that leadership is not about following a list of rules or structures: think of some of the great leaders in history and consider what they achieved and how they did it:

- Alexander the Great, at an age when many of us were still in college, pulled his huge army with him across much of the known world.
- Mahatma Gandi inspired one of the most populous and diverse nations on earth towards a common goal.
- Martin Luther King encouraged the civil rights movement not to give up in the face of almost overwhelming hostility.
- Shackelton led his men across the Antarctic ice, in the face of almost certain catastrophe, when most of them would simply have given up and laid down to die.

None of these men, and others like them, led by force of power or fear, they had a quality that inspired others to do more than they would have expected for themselves. Leadership of young people, however, can be just as great a challenge, if not more. If you are in a formal position of power it is not difficult to force young people to do what you want but this could not be said to be leadership; or if it is, it is an abuse of leadership. Leadership of young people is about finding in yourself a quality that brings out the best qualities of those you work with. It is not about persuasion or coercion, it is not about being in charge or having qualifications or certificates, it is about the challenge of making the right leadership decisions for the right reasons. This book is about that challenge.

So how does this differ from simply working with young people? In essence it is both similar and yet more, when we use the term 'working with' it usually, if not always, implies some element of leadership. It may not be the overt 'follow me' type of leadership, it could just as easily be a facilitative or encouraging type of leadership; but it is leadership. We reserve the right to be leaders working with young people usually because we feel that we have experienced something; or know something; or believe in something that we wish to share. We want to lead others, in this instance young people, into sharing that certain something: it may simply be the knowledge that they don't need us as leaders and there would be nothing wrong with that. Leadership in the context of this book is more than 'working with' young people it is about inspiring or encouraging young people to have the ability to lead themselves to the best of their ability and to meet their full potential (see Chapter 2 Vision and Styles). Leadership of young people also implies taking on a responsibility to the young people themselves and possibly a wider community (see Chapter 14 Rules, Roles and Responsibilities).

On Gender...

It would be remiss if the question of gender were not mentioned here. It will be instantly apparent, and probably some of you are already agitated because of it, that the four leaders mentioned earlier in this introduction were all men. This was not a deliberate move on my part, even though I was very conscious of it, rather it is a reflection of the society that gave rise to our leaders. I could have chosen others such as Mother Teresa or Bernadette of Lourdes but to me these women were not leaders but rather followers who persuaded other people to follow their calling (I know the difference is a debatable one!). Likewise, I could have chosen Joan of Arc, but it would have been hard to separate the myth from the person, I could also have chosen Margaret Thatcher who, leaving political ideology aside, was a great leader in some ways but a poor leader in others. The simple fact is that it is easy to pick out examples of well-known male leadership but less so for female leadership. Despite the fact that so many true leaders 'at the coal face', youth workers, teachers etc. are women, it is still, sadly, the fact that society looks to male role models when it talks about leadership and this is reflected in the hierarchies that surround us. I sincerely hope that nothing in this book reflects this but I apologise if it does. Incidentally, rather than use cumbersome expressions such as s/he or he/she I have chosen to use non-gender specific designations except in cases where there is a reason for doing so.

As for leadership itself; this book discusses the ways in which individual leaders will, and should, develop ways of working unique to themselves. These will naturally be different for men and women, but they will also be different in lots of other ways as well. A good leader will recognise that men and women may lead in different ways, but rather than try to act in a way that is not comfortable or natural for them, they will respect the differences and draw good points from every way of working.

About the Contributors

Peter Barnes is an outdoor education lecturer at the Jordanhill Campus of the University of Strathclyde. He has had a wide and varied career including youth work, military service, radar systems design and many years of outdoor work with Outward Bound and others in a variety of countries. He was also responsible for the instigation and development of outdoor education at the University of Central Lancashire. Following an MA in 'Tourism and Social Responsibility' he completed his PhD in 'The Motivation of Staff Working in the Outdoor Industry'. He has until recently been the chair for the northern region of the Institute for Outdoor Learning and is a Fellow of the Royal Geographical Society. Peter has published widely in a diverse range of subjects revolving around leadership and outdoors. He lives with his partner, Sue, and a manic household of cats and children.

Di Collins has been a teacher and a youth worker, and has been involved with the Duke of Edinburgh's Award for a number of years. She is a member of the Hampshire Outdoor Education Training Team working with teachers and youth workers on the Basic Expedition Leader Award. She also works freelance, often with young people and adults from urban areas, using the outdoors as a vehicle for personal development and a catalyst for community development. She has visited Australia, as a Churchill Fellow, exploring 'other' ways of working particularly with women in and through the outdoors.

Abi Paterson worked at Outward Bound Rhowniar prior to completing a degree and PGCE in Geography. She then taught briefly in mainstream education, and outdoor education. Abi was a Training and Development Manager for Fairbridge for over seven years before recently moving to Gloucestershire LEA as Out of Hours Learning Co-ordinator. 'My time at Fairbridge developed my understanding of people and how they learn: including myself. I am now working with the statutory sector to engage and excite people in the learning process there. My focus has always been on people who find formal learning more difficult: particularly challenging young people. I am currently finding my way around being a Trustee of the Institute of Outdoor Learning and having a new job. I am learning to pace myself better.'

Judy Ling Wong OBE is the Director of Black Environment Network (BEN), an organisation with an international reputation as the pioneer in the field of ethnic participation in the built and natural environment. BEN works across diverse sectors, integrating social, cultural and environmental concerns. Judy is a major voice on policy towards social inclusion. She has worked extensively in various sectors: in the arts, in psychotherapy and in community involvement and currently sits on a number of national task forces and committees relating to the environment and social inclusion. She was made a Fellow of the Royal Society of Arts in 1997 in recognition of her contribution to contemporary environmental thinking. In June 2000 she was appointed an Officer of the Order of the British Empire in recognition of her outstanding contribution to ethnic environmental participation.

Mick Wood began his youth work career as a part-time youth worker in his home town of Liverpool in 1990. He became a nationally qualified youth worker in 2000 whilst undertaking the Youth and Community Work degree course at Derby University. 'Throughout my career I have always had a passion for the outdoors and the use of the outdoor environment as an effective developmental learning tool for young people. This is reflected in the work I do at Endeavour, which provides two-year personal and social development programmes utilising experiential education via, amongst other things, the outdoor experience.' He now lives and works in the Peak District area with his wife Sarah and three young children.

Phil Woodyer has been head of Low Mill Centre for seven years. This centre is a member of the 'Adventure for All' association which promotes outdoor adventure for people with special needs. Previous to his work at Low Mill, Phil was deputy head at Prior House LEA centre and has worked in the outdoor industry for some twenty years. Phil continues to be active in caving, including working as an assessor for the local cave leader scheme. He has also been involved with the Northern Council for Outdoor Education, Training and Recreation as secretary, acted as an external advisor to the University of Central Lancashire, and has published in the areas of working with special needs and outdoor leadership.

Chapter 1

Understanding Young People

Young people is in many ways a cumbersome term, generally the expression youth, or sometimes adolescents, is used as a catch-all term for young people, however it is a term fraught with problems. We live in an age where there is, supposedly, a youth culture, sometimes referred to in the media world as 'yoof'. Unfortunately, no one has been able to satisfactorily decide what 'yoof' actually is. The term remains elusive, widely used and little understood. So who exactly are 'youth'?

Firstly, it would be wrong to blanket such a large group together; young people could include male and female, people from different ethnic groups and all abilities. Chapter 10 'Different Groups, Different Needs covers this but here we need to do that 'wrong' thing and look for a blanket, catch-all, understanding.

Youth as Threat

At one time, in the 1950s, 1960s and even into the 1970s youth culture was regarded with horror by the establishment (another nebulous term), who regarded it as a threat to society's very existence. Young people became, in the words of Davies (1986), 'Threatening Youth'. He described the youth service of this period as being about control and ideology, in other words young people needed to be shown how to behave in a civilised society. If they couldn't or wouldn't respond in a constructive manner then the emphasis moved to 'keeping them off the streets'. Davies (1986: p7) writes that the idea of youth as a group is a socially constructed one that is viewed as threatening because:

> ...its precise meaning and expression have been determined by developments and changing ideas within...society. Through this process, youth has come to be regarded as, by definition, a difficult and even traumatic experience... adolescents as a category have been seen and treated as possessing inherent characteristics; immature, unstable, unreliable...boys...are liable to be aggressive...while girls are moody and withdrawn.

He continues to say that 'neither gender or race, nor class background have been seen as significantly altering any individual's experience of being adolescent'.

Whilst we would hopefully not use blanket terms to condemn such a major group in society today there is still a feeling that 'youth' are outside of society's constraints. The threat has, however, moved from the realm of the political to that of the social. Youth, as Jeffs and Smith (1998: pp50–61) highlight is:

> ...almost exclusively employed to signify discussion of a social problem or behaviour being portrayed in a negative light.

The threat of 'youth' today is thus in their irresponsible and anti-social behaviour, particularly with regard to such areas as sex and drugs (Morrow and Richards, 1996). The 'rave' culture and the, very small, number of deaths caused by the taking of ecstasy, has in the eyes of the media at least, only served to confirm this attitude.

However, as Handy (1993: p55) says:

> *The formation, by the mass media perhaps? of what has come to be called a youth culture with its own norms, values and symbols has presented young people with another, and very powerful, model for their self-concept.*

Whilst all adults may not regard youth culture as a positive thing it is significant that the young people themselves now see this cultural identity as one of their terms of reference.

Age

Age would be an obvious place to start given the term 'young'. However age is such a vague term it indicates nothing but a chronological statistic. Who is a young person? In DfES speak 13–19 years old is young; many charities target 14–25 year olds; increasingly the statutory youth service works with 11–25 year olds. Boys and girls mature at different ages and different people mature, and accept responsibilities at different ages, particularly so in different cultures. If we, as supposedly mature adults, are confused about the age of youth think for a moment about how they feel. They can get married at sixteen but are not responsible enough to vote. Sex is legal at sixteen but not watching a sexual film. A young person can fight and kill for their country, before they are allowed to watch a film rated for violence or are considered mature enough to serve on a jury.

Whilst age could be used as a definition for young people, and indeed for 'official' purposes it often is, it indicates little but a confusion of ideas and serves to do little but confuse the concept of youth. Youth are sometimes under tremendous pressure to act in ways that belie their actual age, for example:

> *The media puts enormous pressure on young people to wear particular clothes, use make-up, listen to this music, watch certain videos and generally behave in a manner beyond their years. This means that they may miss out on the latter part of their childhood and are expected to conform to certain media induced behaviour patterns. It is little wonder then that teenage behaviour often causes conflict.* (Wheal, 1998: p2)

The difficulty is that this conflict lies not only in the way that adults and society perceives young people but also in how young people perceive themselves. Whilst it is certain that age is a biological reality it cannot be construed to be anything more than that, the meaning of youth has little to do with reality, it has more to do with society's perceptions.

Some books on young people tend to categorise this group as belonging to a tight age band; notably the teenage years. This, however, is very restrictive with the differences in maturity and responsibility evident amongst young people. This book, therefore, shies away from placing a particular age band definition on young people other than saying that it is a group that have yet to adopt full adult responsibilities, in other words, as discussed below, a group that is undergoing some form of development.

A Period of Transition

Another way of looking at youth is that young people are at an age where they are in transition between childhood and adulthood or dependency and independence. This then is a period of change but it is also an 'in-between' period. As with the confusion of age this period brings with it a confusion of self-identity.

The problem with transition as an identifying period is that it is nowhere near as clear-cut as it may once have been. Where once there may have been a straight line of moving from childhood to adulthood, usually associated with leaving the family home this line has become increasingly blurred. Indeed it could be argued that the period of transition is now so blurred that it merges into an ongoing continuum of life experience where the only certain points are birth and death. As an example Kiernan (1996, cited in Young, 1999: p25) lists the following as comprising the completion of the transition into adulthood:

- Finishing full-time education.
- Entry into the labour market.
- Leaving home.
- The establishment of an independent household.
- Entry into marriage or cohabitation.
- Parenthood.

Taking these as 'boundary line' events it is clear that they are far from presenting a distinct line between youth and adulthood. Teenage pregnancy is one, increasingly common example where 'adulthood' encroaches into many young lives; unemployment may entail long-term dependency on the family home whilst life-long learning and career changes may mean that many so-called adults will remain engaged in full-time education into their thirties and forties. It may therefore be that adults and youth share strikingly similar issues and problems. Changes in society generally have made transition both more difficult and more fluid. As Maddern (2000: p137) says:

> ...there has been a dramatic erosion of social norms and moral values. The relative certainties of the past have disappeared. The security traditionally offered by work and family, home and community no longer exists.

Moving away from the societal boundary lines to changes within young people themselves Wheal (1998: p6) gives the following as being amongst the changes that they will need help with:

- Finding ways to reconcile their increasing freedom, independence and feelings of maturity with their need to be cared for.
- Growing out of their naïve and somewhat self-centred view of life in order to face some of the difficult realities of the world.
- Integrating their maturing sexual desires and learning to relate to the opposite sex in a more adult manner.
- Making revisions to the way they perceive themselves and others.
- Undergoing changes in their emotional lives that will enable them to handle their feelings more maturely and feel more content and settled inwardly.

It is interesting to note that Wheal does not suggest that young people will need help with becoming responsible and productive members of society. How much those working with young people should fulfil this obligation is a contentious one that has already been touched on and is returned to several times in this book.

It is apparent that if we refer to youth as being a period of transition then Wheal's list is one that can be managed in a much more effective way. This is particularly so if we regard the job of a leader working with young people as being focused on their needs rather than society's. Young (1999: p28) suggests that:

Adolescence is...a moment of questioning—a moment in which young people reflect critically on their sense of self, their beliefs and values.

It is worth taking this as a way forward and positing that youth is not so much about transition or change as about questioning. This is particularly so when the quest for a positive self-identity and self-esteem is considered. As Handy (1993: p55) says 'The self-concept is not formed without trauma. Adolescence is a difficult time'. Despite the changes in society the transition to full adulthood has always been one of questioning and exploration:

Although it is true that we live in a time of bewildering change it is also true that some things remain basically the same. The process of maturation, of growing up, of going from childhood through youth to adulthood is one such unchanging thing. Of course many outer trappings of this period are different, but the fundamental inner journey is essentially the same.
(Maddern, 2000: p138)

This works well for the leader of young people. Because they are in the valuable position of being able to help young people ask, and answer, their questions, they can help lead along that fundamental journey.

Discussion, and a Footnote

What does all this mean for the leader of young people? Firstly that attempting to define 'youth' as a discrete group is a non-starter. The leader working with young people needs to recognise that they should never attempt to categorise youth as a single group. Rather each individual young person or group of young people needs to be approached with a fresh perspective and a fresh approach. There are problems and issues that are common to many young people and these will surface again and again; but they are not problems and issues that are common to *all* young people. Age, despite the obvious link, is of little use as a unifying understanding and neither is the young person's relationship to the society they are in. The notion of youth as a discrete culture is largely society's invention and driven by society's media. Superficially such a culture may appear to exist but there is more to young people than clothes, drugs and music. We can be relatively certain that the great majority of young people will be involved in a journey of discovery but we can also be just as certain that they will all be at different stages on this journey.

This transfers into how we lead young people Ogilvie (1993) makes the point that leaders of young people will adapt their style of leadership (see Chapter 2 Vision and Styles) to the type of group they customarily work with. Thus a Scout leader or Duke of Edinburgh's Award Scheme will see the young people they work with in terms of independency whilst a youth worker or teacher working with remedial young people may possibly tend to think more in levels of dependency. Ogilvie, (1993: p59) suggests that:

Leaders need to be aware that thinking about how they lead can be restricted by the...situation they normally experience. When...different kinds of groups present themselves, ideas about the nature of groups that were previously seen as immutable, are suddenly drastically challenged.

Sadly one of the few commonalities amongst young people is that they will agree that the 'adults' who work with them are old (yes: you!). You might well think you are very far from being old and indeed you may consider yourself a young person, unfortunately they do not see it that way: live with it and respect the difference.

Chapter 2

Vision and Styles

Leadership of any sort is a difficult subject and leadership with young people is harder than most. If we return to the Introduction at the very start of this book it was apparent that defining leadership is very difficult; in this chapter it is how leadership is applied, where power comes from, how much power to use and how to apply leadership that is discussed. Through an understanding of issues such as these it may be possible that a true definition of what leadership is all about can begin to emerge.

Before the question of how to lead can be answered the question of why to lead must be discussed; and the answer to that is in another question; about vision.

Vision

It has been said that leadership is about vision and that leadership without vision is leadership for its own sake. Sharon Wood, the first American woman to reach the top of Everest (cited in Graham, 1997: p16) wrote that:

> *The most important aspect of leadership is having a reason for leading beyond investing in your own ego...always check your intention. Ask yourself why you lead.*

In nearly every occasion that reason for leadership will come down to having some sort of vision of what it is that you hope to achieve as a leader. This vision might be something that you keep to yourself as motivation or it might be something you share in the nature of visionary leadership. Probably the most famous single example of visionary leadership was on the 28th of August, 1963 in Washington DC., Martin Luther King, in the early 1960s, faced the prospect of a faltering civil rights movement divided by internal strife and facing hostile, and often violent, reactions from all sides. Despite this he stood in front of a vast crowd and announced:

> *I say to you today, my friends, that in spite of the difficulties and frustrations of the moment I still have a dream. It is a dream deeply rooted in the American dream. I have a dream that one day this nation will rise up and live out the true meaning of its creed: 'We hold these things to be self-evident; that all men are created equal...'* (quoted in King, 1985: p95)

Martin Luther King not only shared his vision of the future, his 'dream', but he also reminded his audience that his vision was based on the shared vision of the founders of their country: in other words it was everybody's vision. This shared vision united and galvanised the civil rights movement into the society changing force that we remember today.

So why is vision a question? Vision is not only about your work with young people it is also about your honesty with yourself: you need to accept why you want to work with, or 'lead' young people. As Sharon Wood said, you must question your reason for wanting to lead. The answer, if honest, will influence not only how you work but also the sort of work you do. The question then is simple: 'Why do I want to work with young people?'. However, like all simple questions, the answer can lead to more complex debates, for example: 'What can I bring to my work with young people?' and, even more difficult, 'What are my beliefs about working with young people?' When you have answered these questions, and others like them, you will have your own vision to keep yourself going. The next step then is to ask 'Is my vision relevant to the needs, wants and possible vision of the young people that I work with: can I share my vision or do I need to start again from the viewpoint of a young person?'

Working with young people may often require you to take a middle road between idealist and cynic: but you should never lose sight of why you do whatever it is that you do. One difficulty you may encounter is that young people often have no overt vision of their own. This is not to say that all young people are aimless drifters, far from it, but the teenage and young adult years are all about exploration, discovery and often frustration, the vision tends to come later.

Another consideration when it comes to vision is to be realistic:

> When I was a newly qualified teacher I was seriously expecting a glamorous life, filled with moments of learning breakthroughs and touching pastoral Dead Poet's Society hugs and personal revelations. It took me about three months to realise that this was total garbage, and if I wanted my working life to mean anything it would be because Darren actually remembered his homework diary after two weeks of persuasion.   (Warren, 2001: p48)

This is not to say that a leader's vision should not be idealistic, just that a healthy dose of realism will be helpful when it comes to the up and downs of working with young people. You may find this frustrating but remember one golden rule: you can share your vision, but you should never impose it on others: working with young people is about education not indoctrination. A leader of young people does not lead them into an imposed vision but provides opportunities for them to find their own vision for themselves.

Judgement, Negligence and Responsibility

One aspect that is at the core of leadership is the need for a leader to exercise judgement. This is usually taken as the ability to make decisions based on experience, knowledge, qualification, personal skill and 'gut instinct'. Judgement is at the heart of all leadership decisions and is often only acquired through making mistakes and learning from them. More than anything else it is this aspect of leadership that requires experience and maturity.

Judgement is, in many ways, the hardest aspect of leadership to master precisely because of its intangible nature. A legal clue to the nature of judgement can be found in the concept of negligence which was defined, in 1856, as:

> ...the omission to do something which a reasonable man would do, or doing something which a prudent and reasonable man would not do.   (Tayfor, 1995: p12)

Although poor judgement could not be considered negligence, which is a legal term implying not only harm to a person but also a duty of care being owed to a person, it does give a good starting point. Essentially judgement could be considered as taking all the facts at your disposal, using your experience to have a good guess at the facts you don't know and then deciding whether what you want to do would be the action of a 'prudent and reasonable man' (whatever that might be!) rather than that of a negligent one.

Obviously the biggest unknown when working with young people is usually the possible action of the young people themselves: you might think you have all the angles covered and then the people in your care do something completely unexpected. This is where experience and 'expecting the unexpected' come into play. It is important, however, to always recognise the legal implications of your judgement: young people, especially younger children cannot, in the eyes of the law, be expected to act reasonably. This means that even if, in your judgement, you could trust the young people involved to act in a certain way and they do something else which resulted in them being harmed it is you who is at fault and not them.

A starting point in the building of sound judgement is an understanding of the nature of leadership.

The Bases of Power

Before leadership can be fully understood, however, it is well to appreciate where the power to be a leader comes from, it is very often the application of this power that marks a leader's way of working. Leaders generally, very generally, fall into two types; emergent and prescribed, the first of these simply means leaders who have emerged from their peers because of some exceptional trait whilst the second are those who are leaders because they have been designated as such. Whatever the type of leader there are five primary sources of power, known as the bases of power (Raven and Rubin, 1975). These power bases are:

- resource (or reward)
- expert
- legitimate
- charisma (or referent)
- coercive

Resource power

The essence of resource power is that the leader has it within their power to give some form of reward. In an industrial or business context this power base can be the ability to provide, and increase or decrease, wages, promotion and ultimately employment itself. The resources controlled by the leader of young people can be as tangible as the type of activity provided or more subtle rewards such as praise or approval. The rewards do, of course, have to have value in the eyes of the young people involved. It has also been found that non-specific rewards to a group in general only have a short-term effect, to be effective in the long term rewards must be both personal and specific.

Expert power

This is often the most acceptable form of power because people are able to rationalise why the 'expert' is in charge. For expert power to work the young people involved must acknowledge and respect that a person has the necessary expertise. This is the reason why bluffing to cover up for a lack of knowledge almost inevitably ends up with loss of control over a group. A problem with expert power is that the person involved may only be an expert in one field and unable to incorporate or delegate others, they therefore become isolated and function solely as an expert rather than as a leader. However, it is also worth noting that extremely high levels of expert power are transferable: a top footballer, for example, would be respected by young boys, and expected to be successful, whatever the activity involved.

Legitimate power

There are two sources of legitimate power; nominated and democratic. Nominated power implies some form of moral authority conferred in the leader. This will usually be the group leader with the power conferred in them by virtue of the job. Democratic power is where a group of people have elected a leader for various possible reasons. It is important to note that legitimate, sometimes known as position, power can be hard to maintain, in many cases it relies on being able to call on one or more of the other forms of power base, such as expert power. It is absolutely vital that people who have legitimate power invested in them never give way to the 'because I said so and I'm in charge' type of leadership or they will soon find themselves out of power! The prescribed leader will always have some form of legitimate power to call on.

Charisma power

This is perhaps the most sought after, and the most abused, form of power. The reason for this is that charisma power is seen as a validation of the person rather than the position. The source of charismatic power is in the personality of the person wielding it. This personality need not be loud; a calm manner can often be a vital asset allowing this type of leader to act as an effective co-ordinator. People who lack true charisma power, but aspire to it, are prone to dominate, rather than lead, the group through loudness or physical presence. At its best this type of domination is disruptive and at its worst can be highly counter-productive. The great emergent leaders in history have usually been associated with charisma. Charisma power is at its most influential when others compare, or refer, their actions against the standards and actions of the leader. For this reason, if nothing else, it is important that the leader maintains high personal standards.

Coercive power

This power base tends to be the opposite of the other bases listed above. Essentially it is power through threat or domination usually involving the use of negative incentive such as avoiding punishment or ridicule. Often tried when resource power has failed, expert power is inapplicable, charisma power is not present and legitimate power is threatened, the use of coercive power is never a long-term solution. Whilst immediate tasks might be completed successfully there will be no long-term motivation to develop or perform well. This is similar to the action/reaction communication model (Chapter 4) where although the action might be positive the reaction is negative. For example, the task gets successfully completed but resentment is built up about the manner in which the task was led.

What are the implications of the bases of power for leading with young people? Young people will usually automatically assume that the leader is more experienced and more capable than them, that they have a degree of expert power. However this is often the least important of the bases of power. For example, a leader does not need to know the rules of football; they can delegate the referee's job to one of the young people and merely keep an eye on the conduct of the game. This can be done because normally the leader has a legitimate power base simply because they are 'the leader', they may well, however, need to call on charisma power if there are 'characters' in the group who need either winning over or reassuring. Finally resource power is the ultimate trump card where if things are not working out the leader always has the power to reward success, in whatever criteria are being used. Young people should not, however, be encouraged to succeed purely with the objective of gaining a reward; they should be 'steered' towards the intrinsic reward of pride or self-satisfaction. This is a far more effective system in the long term. Rarely, if ever, is coercive power of any use other than in the immediate short term and even then only in a task oriented situation.

Leadership Styles

Although the two are closely linked, to a large extent the essence of good leadership lays not so much in how power is applied but in the style of leadership adopted. These can be summed up by Figure 1, based on the work of Tannerbum and Schimdt (1973).

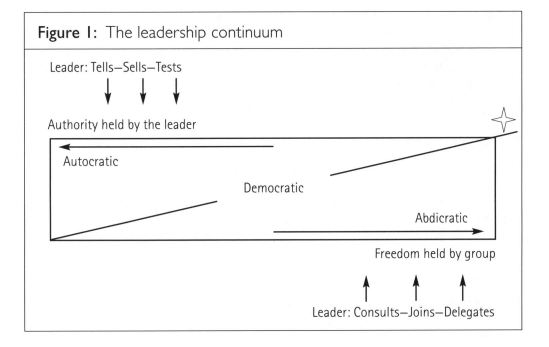

Figure 1: The leadership continuum

Leader: Tells—Sells—Tests

Authority held by the leader

Autocratic

Democratic

Abdicratic

Freedom held by group

Leader: Consults—Joins—Delegates

This figure makes it clear that at the left of the continuum the leader enjoys total, autocratic, leadership. This is usually a very safe style of leadership but can be stifling for those you are working with. At the other extreme the leader has abdicated leadership and the group is allowed to make its own mistakes. There is a time and a place for this style of leadership as much as for autocratic leadership, however it can quickly lead to unsafe or out of control situations. It may seem as if the ideal is a position somewhere between these two extremes but the truth is that the amount of leadership a good leader displays can be swinging back and forwards on an almost constant basis. A quick litany describing the leadership continuum is that, going from left to right of the model, the leader tells, sells, tests, consults, joins and delegates. These actions or roles can be split into three pairings which give an indication of the broad leadership style: autocratic (telling and selling), democratic (test and consulting) and abdicratic (joining and delegating).

It is worth looking at the leadership roles in some detail because we can base the whole discussion of the nature of leadership on them:

Autocratic — tells

The leader is making all the decisions; they have set themselves up as the expert who knows best. This style of leadership is very effective for task oriented activities (see Chapter 3 Action centred leadership) where there is no room or time for flexibility or discussion, the military or emergency services would be a good example of this. This style of leadership does not, however, allow any room for personal growth because it stifles initiative and creativity.

Autocratic — sells

The leader continues to make the decisions as before except this time the group are encouraged to agree with that decision by the leader sharing the reason the decision was made. This gives the impression of engaging the group and does make them more involved but it is a largely cosmetic exercise as the leader is still the only one empowered to make decisions. This style of leadership does, however, allow for some personal growth because the group can understand the reasoning behind a course of action.

Democratic — tests

Again a stage further in engaging the group with the decision making process. In this style the leader addresses the concerns of the group by answering questions regarding people's concerns. The power of the final decision rests with the leader but the group are able to raise objections or queries that the leader may take into consideration. The group are therefore engaged in the process to the extent that their concerns have been taken into account.

Democratic — consults

Whilst the leader still remains the final arbiter of any decision, the group are given the chance to engage with the decision making process through direct input. The leader presents the scenario involved and puts the options to the group along with the possibility of the group bringing more options into play. Personal growth is therefore enhanced by the young people being given the option of contributing to the discussion, even if, ultimately, they have a limited ability to determine the final decision.

Abdicratic — joins

This is a consensual decision making process with the leader presenting the scenario and any information plus possible decisions and then engaging in a genuine exchange of ideas. The final decision in this style is a joint decision made with the group and leader on equal terms. Personal growth is therefore fostered to a large extent with the leader playing a facilitating role as much as a leadership role.

Abdicratic — delegates

In this final style the leader presents the scenario but then steps back entirely leaving the group to arrive at its own decisions remaining present only for consultation and guidance if necessary. This style of leadership has the maximum potential for growth but it also has the maximum potential for negative growth or regression if the group are not ready to take on this kind of responsibility or if one or two members of the group assume full responsibility, dominate the group or disrupt it in other ways. Even when the power to make decisions has been delegated the leader should maintain a 'watching brief' to ensure that growth is being engendered and also to ensure that whatever is happening is safe. Whilst the aim of any leader should be to hand over as much power as is sensible and appropriate they must always be in a position to grab it back as soon as it is necessary. The prime rule to remember when handing over the authority to make decisions is: 'Authority can be delegated but responsibility never can.'

Abdication

There is a final style of leadership, which is off to the right of the continuum (the 'star' symbol in Figure 1). This is total abdication where the leader delegates all authority and responsibility. This can arise through a deliberate policy of delegation or through a leader losing control. In either case it is never a suitable style of leadership when working with young people. Even when the young people are out of the direct control of the leader, such as on a Duke of Edinburgh's Award expedition, the leader should still be able to monitor the progress of the group, even if only sporadically, and be in a position to assume responsibility for its actions.

Another way of looking at the leadership styles is not in the power being exercised over the decision making process but in the relationship of the leader to the group. The two opposing relationship styles, based on a theme developed by Phil Woodyer (unpublished) can be summed up as shown in Figure 2.

These roles may often seem contradictory but should rather be viewed as complimentary and switched between as appropriate. It is worth asking where you fit into these roles when working as a leader with young people.

Are you an 'ego man' dragging all and sundry along with you to do what you want to do, to impress your party with your vast feats of daring, your immunity to pain and cold water and

---

Figure 2: Relationship styles

Ego man		**Friendly advisor**
Leading light		Guiding light
Dictator	**vs**	Educator
Leader		Shepherd

your vast knowledge? Or are you the 'friendly adviser', leading by suggestion, guiding your party to self-discovery and self-awareness? 'Ego man' may impress many of his party but will not interest many of them in the activity in question unless his ego is tempered with a certain amount of sympathy for the needs and concerns of the party. 'Friendly advisor' may well switch his party on to what they are doing and the environment around them, but he may also switch them off permanently if at certain times he does not assert his authority when danger or chaos threaten.

Both relationship styles are extremes rather than mainstream ways of working, but both have their place. In general terms, for example, a youth football team would do well being coached by 'ego man' but rather less well if run by 'friendly advisor' whereas a drugs counselling group would go nowhere with 'ego man' in charge. This theme of the relationship between the young people and the leader is developed in more detail in the next chapter.

Developing a Unique Way of Working

No doubt you would argue that you do not entirely fit into either side of the leadership styles or the relationship tables and this is as it should be. A person's style of leadership grows from their personality and there are elements of these extremes in all of us. Good leadership comes from knowing when to use appropriate styles and techniques, with which individuals and groups and in which situations. A leader will also have their own unique way of working which is over and above the styles identified so far in this chapter. It may be that one person leads everything they do in a very precise and ordered manner whilst another person prefers a more chaotic, spur of the moment style. Likewise one leader may find it very easy to be friendly with young people whilst another may prefer to be a little more detached. Leadership, as mentioned in the Introduction to this book, is not about following a list of rules or structures; rather it is about a combination of heart and head. People skills, as opposed to technical skills, are often more about 'gut reactions' and feelings than they are about following the 'correct' pattern of working.

A leader should never try to conceal their own personality and character because not only would such a façade be impossible to maintain but young people would quickly judge such a leader to be false. A good leader will recognise the strengths and weaknesses of the way they work and act on them in a positive manner, working always to their strengths whilst accommodating their weaknesses. This is one reason why role models are valuable but a leader needs to be able to learn from them rather than emulate them. As Paul Petzoldt, the founder of the National Outdoor Leadership School in America (cited in Graham, 1997: p18) says: 'Leadership is not just passed on from the more experienced to the less experienced'. There are many ways that a leader will learn, from others, from experience, from books and courses; and from making mistakes. Ultimately all of these routes will need to be incorporated into one whole that has at its foundation the personality and character of the person involved (see Chapter 13 Measuring Success).

Your Way of Working: *Activity*

An interesting, and usually fun, way to explore how your personality and character impact on the way you work is through the use of metaphors. This can be done as a light-hearted game or it can be taken much deeper (as always, however, be aware of exposing emotions and feelings that cannot be resolved). In a group take it in turns to describe each other, in terms of whatever attribute you wish to discuss, as another object. For example:

- If your way of leading was a car, it would be a slick sports car because you are always rushing straight into things without thinking about the consequences but for some reason everyone loves the way you work, or
- If your personality was a tree it would be an oak because you are so solid and dependable, we know we can always rely on you whatever the storm.

This game can also be done with young people as a friendly way of getting them to talk about each other.

Leadership and Spirituality 'Minus the Loaves and Fishes': *Mick Wood*

When you hear the word *leadership* you may find yourself bombarded with images of the likes of Shackleton or Hunt battling against the odds, men of great achievements and, undoubtedly, great examples of good leadership. However, is this what we mean by *leadership* in today's society? Is leadership meant only for those on adventurous endeavours? I would suggest it is not: leadership is not constrained to men nor expeditions of great adventures but is a valuable tool for all in everyday social interaction.

If it is, indeed, an important aspect of social life, what constitutes effective leadership? It was this question that lead me on to looking deeper into the make up of good, effective leadership.

During an innovative, multi-organisational, leadership program at the end of September 2000 the identification of separate aspects of leadership became apparent to me. The three aspects of an effective leader, I suggest , are:

Experience

Without entering into the intellectual arguments of experience and knowledge, whether metaphysical or epistemological (as talked about by the likes of Dewey, see Chapter 8), for the purpose of this piece I simply define experience as the sum of the engagement an individual has with the outside world, in all it's forms.

Hard skills

These are the technical knowledge and competencies needed to perform specific tasks. An example of this can be taken from John Adair (see Chapter 3) and his model of action centred leadership (which uses the same graphical representation as the model being described) through to the ability to tie knots, facilitate a group etc.

Spiritual awareness

This is an intangible aspect and as such is difficult to define, although many writers have tried. The following attempt comes some way to getting close:

> *Spirituality is defined as an altered state of consciousness where an individual may experience a higher sense of self, inner feelings, inner knowledge, awareness and attainment to the world and one's place in it, knowledge of personal relationships and the relationship to the environment, or a belief in a power greater than imaginable.* (Fox, 2000: p455)

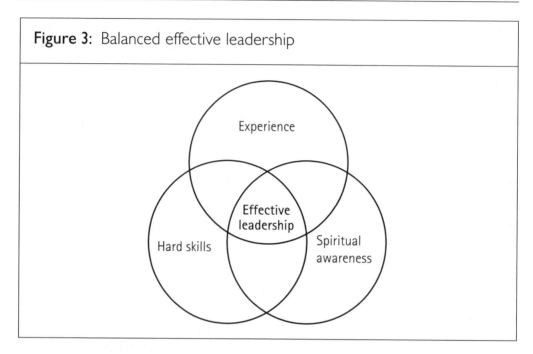

Figure 3: Balanced effective leadership

These three main aspects form the leadership triad and are to be developed equally in order to increase the central area, the area of 'effective leadership' (see Figure 3).

Each 'sphere' of the triad can be developed independently, and almost infinitely, but it is the development of all the spheres that will increase the effective leadership skills of an individual. In Figure 4 we can see what happens to the area of effective leadership when one of the spheres of the triad is developed independently of the others.

Whilst that specific aspect is developed the effective leadership ability of the individual is not significantly increased, it is only when all spheres of the triad are developed that this will happen. This does not have to happen all at the same time but equal consideration must be given to all aspects in order to develop an individual's leadership ability. This model of leadership firmly stands in the 'leaders are made and not born' camp although it does recognise that certain individuals may be born with a natural aptitude for one or more of these leadership aspects and could then be perceived as a 'natural' leader, i.e. 'born not made'.

So, what exactly is 'spirituality'?

As discussed earlier, *spirituality* to many is an elusive term, we all believe we know what it is but we can't exactly put our finger on a definitive answer to *what is spirituality*. To me, spirituality is a very personal thing and will be many things to many people and, as such, spiritual experiences will take many forms. To some this will be in relation to the natural world, to others it will be the camaraderie between friends or participation in physical activity. Whatever the catalyst the experience itself shares many attributes (Stringer and McAvoy, 1992, cited by Fox, 2000: p458):

- The shared or common spirit between and among people.
- A power or authority greater than self.
- Clarity of inner or self-knowledge.

- Inner feelings (especially of peace, oneness and strength).
- Awareness and attainment to the world and one's place in it.
- The way in which one relates to fellow humans and to the environment.
- Intangibility.

Figure 4: Un-balanced effective leadership

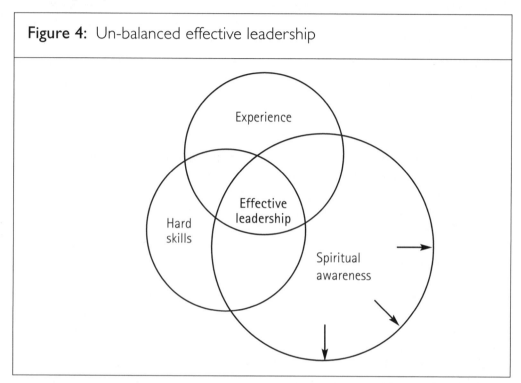

The very last attribute highlights the difficulty in providing any description, *intangibility.* The interesting point, in relation to spirituality and leadership, is 'Awareness and attainment to the world and one's place in it.' This attribute alone will provide young leaders with a whole host of skills to better fulfil any leadership role they may have. To many readers the term 'spirituality' may well raise the hairs on the back of their necks with the flush of memories about the almighty and eternal damnation for their sins or other doctrines of organised religion. This will happen just as readily to young people if you confront them with a session dedicated to *developing your spirituality*, but this needn't be the case:

> *An important point to remember about spirituality is that it is not synonymous with religious experience.* (McDonald and Schreyer, 1991, cited by Fox, 2000: p455)

So it is with this point in mind that spirituality is best approached for the majority of young people. Relating spirituality to the everyday lives of young people and not to any predetermined religion will have a much more profound effect upon them and their future roles. Many young people will have barriers towards the 'S' word but these are not barriers that cannot be surmounted. If you were to ask young people to describe a truly happy moment for them, they would all have a moment they could share (some easier than others!). It could be argued that this is a spiritual moment, a period of contentment with their world, a sense of belonging and purpose. Even with this choice of words I am falling back into an old trap of spirituality, language. The use of clichés in the description of anything spiritual will lead young people's barriers shooting back up and leave you in a position to start from scratch.

When asked what makes a good leader many young people will skirt around the issue of spirituality and may dress it up in 'socially accepted' language. In modern day youth work self-awareness and self-understanding are key to the development of young people, empowerment is the key word of the moment. Therefore this may be the language they choose to use when describing a spiritual aspect. Spiritual understanding is recognised by young people:

> *A good leader is someone who is on the same level as you. Someone who can easily make friends and has an understanding of you, as well as themselves. They should be honest and let you know the limitations.* (18 year old volunteer for Endeavour)

Essentially what they are saying is that an effective leader understands themselves, who they are, and how they work, as well as others around them, and the link between the two.

So, with the characteristics of spirituality being identified as important aspects of a good leader by young people themselves, and in their own choice of language, we should feel more confident of promoting and developing the understanding of spirituality in young people, and it's link to leadership. Go out and explore spirituality in detail, find spirituality in as many different forms as possible. Art, music, discussion, nature and relationships they all hold different aspects of spirituality we just need to feel confident in approaching these activities on a new level, with the view of relating spiritual understanding to effective leadership. Promote it as an individual understanding, which will be different for everyone, and not as some predetermined set of rules that every young person *has* to buy into and follow dogmatically. Freedom is the key to spiritual understanding; let young people find their own spirituality in their own time, not forced by time constraints etc. With careful and skilful facilitation, and review, of any situation it can be capitalised upon to develop this deeper understanding of themselves. Remember that you, as well as the young person, must practice this freedom in your approach after all you are aiming to be an effective leader as well! Be confident in yourself and your abilities to explore spirituality with the risk it carries of getting things wrong. Take that journey together and explore your own spirituality with the young person, remember the words of the young person earlier 'a good leader is someone who is on the same level as you'.

The Role of Leadership

In essence, leadership styles, and the use of particular styles, reflects the discussion on the role of the leader working with young people. This role is far from clear-cut. Graham (1997: p12) gives a good starting point for the discussion of what being a leader is all about when he writes that:

> *Good leaders sometimes tell people what to do, but leadership is not just giving directions: it's liberating people to do what's needed in the best possible way...Leadership is the capacity to move others towards goals shared with you, with a focus and competency they would not achieve on their own.*

This highlights that leadership is about helping others to achieve their goals, although whether it is essential, as Graham implies, that those goals are shared between the young people and the leader is a debatable issue. However, if these goals are purely physical, the development of a new youth club facility for example, then the leadership style could remain completely autocratic and the goal would be achieved. This, however, is surely not what leading young people is all about. The goal of the leader working with young people may be overtly the completion of a physical task but the true agenda in the majority of cases is realising the true potential of the young people involved (see Chapter 5 Motivating Young People).

The aim of a leader is to move along the leadership continuum from autocratic to abdicratic, giving young people the skills needed to make their own decisions and their own way in life. This, of course, can lead to conflict where the leadership style may be appropriate in the eyes of the leader's vision and way of working but inappropriate in the eyes of outsiders. A current dilemma for example, at the time of writing, would be the smoking of cannabis; many young people (and indeed many older people) see this as perfectly normal and acceptable whilst 'society' has deemed it to be illegal. At the time of writing the legal status of cannabis was being reviewed with the intention to downgrade it to a non-arrestable level. However, this example still serves as a good indication of the sort of dilemma that leaders working with young people may have to face. Do you enforce the legislation or do you turn a blind eye to what is happening; do you constrain or educate, oppose or agree? Wheal (1998: p15) highlights dilemmas such as this and also brings up problems which might be perceived as hypocrisy on the part of the leader:

> *Adults who take drugs, even socially, may have a problem with being...dogmatic and must reconcile their own behaviour against that which is best for the young person. What is important is that young people have all the information available and understand the risks and possible dangers.*

As always: for truly effective leadership of young people there are few definitive, or prescriptive, guidelines. The approach and style both depend on the people and circumstances involved. The ultimate personal guideline will always involve a combination of vision, judgement and 'what is right in the circumstance'. This leads us into leadership orientation, the next chapter.

> *On expedition I learned a lot of new skills and it has helped me to improve a lot of things such as my leadership. We took turns to be 'day leader'; someone who is in charge of the day. At first I found it really hard because you had to tell people to do things they didn't want to. You had to keep people motivated and keep them going which was hard at times, but through the ten weeks it got easier to do. I also learned to be more tolerant.*
> (Andriene Smith, 18 year old Raleigh International participant, quote taken from the 'A Question of Balance' conference, 29/11/00)

Chapter 3

Leadership Orientation

A progression from looking at levels and styles of leadership is to look at how leadership is delivered dependant on the circumstances prevailing at the time: in other words the leadership orientation. To examine this we first need to look at what leadership affects and what it needs to take into account. One of the most popular ways of doing this is through the 'action centred leadership' model of John Adair.

Action Centred Leadership

In essence this model (Adair, 1988a; 1988b) shows that there are three aspects to effective leadership which must interact: the point at which the circles cross, before that leadership can be said to be truly effective. These aspects are achieving the task, developing each individual within the team and building and reinforcing the team spirit and teamwork. This is usually demonstrated by the three circle model shown in Figure 5.

The reason for these three aspects can be seen as the chained need, or aim, to achieve a task through the use of a team of people who are all individuals. The effective leader needs to address each aspect, usually simultaneously; if one aspect takes priority then the other two still need to be maintained. As each circle overlaps it can be seen how lack of attention to any one aspect would be to the detriment of the other two.

It is worth noting however, that in the three circle model the task is uppermost, thereby giving it priority. This reflects the model's function of demonstrating leadership skills in a managerial/military setting; obviously in an educative or facilitative setting such as in leadership with young people this would not always be the case (see discussion at the end of this chapter as well as Chapter 2). The key actions involved in action centred leadership are shown in Figure 6.

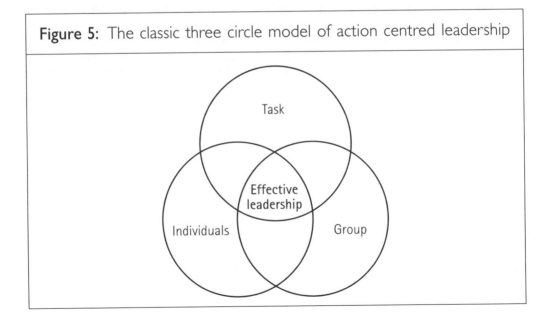

Figure 5: The classic three circle model of action centred leadership

Figure 6: The key actions of action centred leadership (Adair, 1988b: p33)

Key actions	Task	Team	Individual
Define objectives	Identify tasks and constraints	Involve team Share commitment	Clarify objectives Gain acceptance
Plan	Establish priorities Check resources Decide Set standards	Consult Encourage ideas and actions Develop suggestions Structure	Assess skills Set targets Delegate
Brief	Brief the team Check understanding	Answer questions Obtain feedback	Listen Enthuse
Support and monitor	Report progress Maintain standards Discipline	Co-ordinate Reconcile conflict	Advise Assist Recognise effort Counsel
Evaluate	Summarise progress Review objectives Re-plan if needed	Recognise success Learn from failure	Assess performance Appraise Guide, train and develop

In addition to its leadership function, action centred leadership is a useful indicator of good teamwork because it reflects the fact that a team going about a task is made up of individuals and the same three aspects need to be addressed.

Action centred leadership, although primarily a managerial leadership model, is also a useful generic model and can be applied to leadership with young people. It demonstrates that leadership is not complete unless all three aspects are at least considered. To use a very glib example if your job is to coach a junior football team but you spend the whole session working with one of the team who has problems with a particular skill the team will not only fall apart but they won't learn the set-piece that was the object of the session. If however, you concentrate exclusively on practising the set-piece very little team spirit will be developed and your troubled individual will be left even more isolated. Finally, you could spend the entire session running team-bonding activities that neglect the task, the set-piece, and the individuals within the team. To be effective as a leader in this session you need to be able to get the team working together, build up individual skills and make every member of the team feel valued and work on the set-piece practice. In the managerial, task uppermost, model it would be the set-piece practice that would take priority but as a leader working with young people it might be that, although the set-piece will still be practised, concentrating on team spirit may be the uppermost aspect or priority.

Situational Leadership

The concept of situational leadership, devised by Hersey and Blanchard (1982), suggests that leadership needs to take more than the three elements of action centred leadership into account. It suggests that the style of leadership, as in Chapter 2, needs to take into account the 'task' and the 'relationship' of those involved. These dimensions need to be considered as below:

The task: Has to be gauged for its relative importance, not only in terms of its difficulty but also in terms of its importance to the group involved. Is the task complex in relationship to the skills available to complete it and is the effort needed worthy of the likely outcome? (see also Chapter 5 Motivating Young People).

The relationship: Needs to be considered for the quality of the working relationship amongst the group involved as well as the abilities of the group. This would include such aspects as their coherence, motivation and ability to sustain the task.

The leadership style: Will vary dependant on the interaction of the first two dimensions. This model uses four leadership styles, authoritarian, adaptive/flexible, participatory and delegatory. These styles broadly sit on the same autocratic, democratic, abdicratic scale used in the Tannerbum and Schmidt model discussed in Chapter 2.

The correlation between the task, the relationship of those involved and the leadership style can be summed up as in Figure 7.

1. High Task/Low Relationship – authoritarian leadership style

This situation would come about where a group is just getting used to each other (see Chapter 6 The stages of team development) and there is uncertainty regarding the abilities and skills held by individuals within the group. The task, which may in reality be quite simple, can seem daunting because of the group's own uncertainty. It is usually important at this stage for a leader to engineer a success for the group so that they have a foundation to build on. The leader will, therefore, be quite directive in terms of both completing the task and directing the group interaction. Individual and group learning and development in this situation will usually be minimal although morale and motivation may be boosted.

The other circumstance in which this situation might come about is where there is an emergency and completion of the task involved takes priority over any group development or interaction.

2. High Task/High Relationship – adaptive or flexible leadership style

The essence of the leadership style in this instance is that it needs to be able to respond to circumstances. This is because although the task dimension is high, meaning that it has both an element of difficulty and importance, the nature of the group relationship means that they will need to resolve issues and difficulties for themselves. The relationship between group members is tied into the completion of the task so that if they lose coherence or direction the probability of success in the task is unlikely. The leader, therefore, needs to be able to stand back and allow the considerable learning and development that is going on to take place but be ready to step in if the circumstances require outside facilitation or direction.

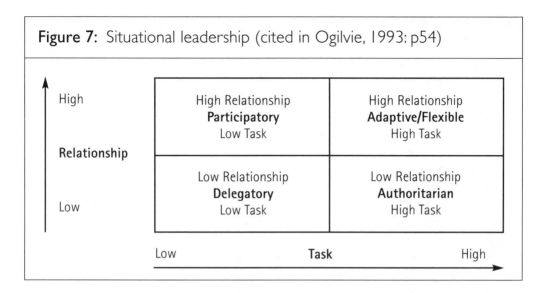

Figure 7: Situational leadership (cited in Ogilvie, 1993: p54)

3. Low Task/High Relationship – participatory leadership style

In this situation the group are able to cope with the task without the intervention of outside help or leadership. They have generally developed enough to be aware of the skills and abilities available within the group and, furthermore, should be able to resolve any difficulties they encounter. The leader will now be able to allow the task dimension to resolve itself whilst remaining involved with the group to ensure that individual and group learning within the group is maximised. For example, they might suggest ways of working which fully utilise all members of the group. The leader does need to ensure that they move away from direct leadership of the group in this situation.

4. Low Task/Low Relationship – delegatory leadership style

Here because the task dimension is low, either because it is simple or the consequences are not important, the leader is able to take on a role that will directly foster group and individual development. To this end the leader will be delegating tasks but allowing the group, and individuals within the group, to carry out the task unsupervised. The learning involved therefore, is less about the successful completion of a delegated task but more about how the task was undertaken.

Caring Leadership

Given that this book is about leadership with young people it is important to consider how the young person is involved in the orientation of leadership and its priorities. This links this chapter on orientation to the previous chapter on leadership styles, particularly with regard to caring leadership; in other words leadership which puts the individual young person first.

In Chapter 14, the discussion on responsibilities makes the point that this focus, which most leaders working with young people would see as a priority, is in many ways the easiest responsibility to neglect. Caring leadership is one very important way of addressing this balance in that it allows a leader to respond to a variety of needs and adopt the range of leadership styles but without losing sight of the individual young person.

Caring leadership is about more than simply focusing on the needs of the young people in your charge, it is about being able to relate to them as people and being able to empathise with their problems and feelings. Evans (cited in Graham, 1997: p70) suggests that the first step towards being able to do this is:

> ...*you have to be vulnerable. You can't put yourself on a pedestal. You must be accessible to the people around you, making them understand that you're human too.*

Building on this it is also important that the leader regards the young people involved as individuals in their own right and that, as Wheal (1998: pp82–83) says:

> ...*caring about someone arises from respect for them as a person and, if we get to know them as a person, usually develops into valuing them as a people...creating an environment which extends young people's development entails adults providing a range of experiences, including opportunities to act individually and in groups, to lead and to follow, and to take risks. Giving responsibilities and setting expectations which enhance a young person's sense of self-worth are likely to reassure a young person that they are cared about...*

Caring leadership requires that the leader demonstrates a higher than usual level of attributes such as sensitivity, time, energy and commitment. It means that you cannot be the sort of leader who regards the leadership of young people as simply a job; it must have an extra dimension which lifts it above that. The main features of caring leadership include (Graham, 1997: p75; Wheal, 1998: p38):

- Putting yourself in others' shoes and being sensitive to their needs.
- Being vulnerable...sharing personal experiences of your own.
- Listening, demonstrate caring by active, non-judgemental listening.
- Explaining to young people what you are doing and what you would expect them to do.
- Setting clear boundaries and expectations.
- Putting caring into action, letting young people know that you will work for their benefit.
- Following through, caring is about forming and maintaining relationships.
- Letting go of judgement and acknowledging young people as individuals.
- Caring for beginners.
- Correcting with caring, try to correct in private.
- Acknowledging others for their achievements, strengths and contributions.
- Demonstrating respect for young people, not least by saying *please* and *thank-you*.

The notion of caring leadership essentially means that the leader puts the needs of the individual young person at the forefront of their priorities. This may well require a delicate balancing act with the needs of the individual being balanced against the needs of the group. However, one advantage of this way of working is that it will, in time, become a two-way process. Once the young people that you work with realise that you genuinely care about them a bond of trust will be formed which will permeate throughout the work you are engaged in. This should mean that if a group activity is stopped to allow a less able person to catch up, the group will respond in a positive manner because they can appreciate the reasons behind the action. It is often only when caring leadership is present that groups of young people can genuinely work together and act to resolve conflict amongst themselves. Greenaway (1996: p21) suggests that good reviewing (see Chapter 9 Reviewing and Feedback) is a feature of caring leadership:

> By reviewing activities we show that we care about what young people experience; that we value what they have to say; and that we are interested in the progress of each individual's learning and development. But it should not just be the reviewer who demonstrates these attitudes: ideally the whole group should reflect them: especially if it is an influential peer group.

Clearly caring leadership, if seen through to its natural fulfilment, will make your work as a leader easier and allow you to spot any potential problems that might have remained hidden if a bond of trust did not allow people to be open. It will also help the progress of the ideal of a leader working with young people, that they should start to take responsibility for their own learning and welfare, looking after each other rather than always looking to the leader to help out.

Obviously this is very idealistic but there is no reason why this approach to working with young people should not be attempted. In summary it can be seen that caring leadership is as much about your relationship as a person to young people as it is about your relationship to them as a leader. Being sensitive to their needs, listening to their problems without being judgemental and acting on issues and problems which are bought forward are all symbolic of a healthy relationship. Whilst this approach to leadership orientation might seem as if it must operate at the democratic or abdicratic end of the leadership continuum (previous chapter Leadership styles) this is not the case. Caring leadership is a way of working that can run through the whole spectrum of leadership styles; there is no reason why an autocratic leader should not also be caring. Indeed this would, on occasions, be a logical way of working with young people who, for whatever reason, are not yet ready to make decisions for themselves.

The Focus of Leadership

It is important to remember that the focus, or orientation, of leadership can change in an instant to match changing circumstances and that, furthermore, the focus might not actually be on the overt object of the exercise. As an example, Ogilvie (1993: p68) tells this story:

> *A morning meeting that was making decisions about the programme for the day was disrupted by the intrusion of events in the recent history of the group. Earlier on, a lot of resentment had arisen around the table-tennis table about whose turn it was to play next. A lively exchange was now being allowed to take place which became a matter of fierce argument about whether the winner of the previous game always earned the right to be one of the players in the next game or whether it should be a completely different pair. An important issue for them about fairness and justice was at stake. If left unresolved it would have serious effects on the harmony and cohesion of the group and the achievement of their aims. The priorities of an authoritarian regime concerned about getting on with the activities might have swept the whole thing under the carpet as an irrelevant side issue: with untold consequences.*

Ogilvie goes on to relate how the task element, planning the activities, was put on hold to address a different set of priorities to do with group cohesion and individual rights as well as personal learning and development. He concludes by saying that: 'If this episode is read as putting table-tennis before more important matters, the whole point has been missed. 'What happened in this example is that the focus of leadership had moved from the task dimension to the group and individual dimensions, if this had not happened the task dimension might have been placed in jeopardy at a later date. More importantly, however, it was considered that the group and individual dimensions were considered at that stage to be of a greater priority. It is evident that the change of focus in leadership also entailed a change in the leadership style which had been authoritarian, working with a low relationship group and a high task dimension, planning the activities. This moved to an adaptive/flexible style in order to facilitate the group resolving an issue within itself. It can be seen, therefore, how leadership focus and orientation is frequently reflected in the style of leadership adopted.

In this example caring leadership is also evident through addressing the concerns, and needs, of the group ahead of the needs of the programme. Again it can be seen how this caring approach is not to the detriment of the task but will actually enhance the ability of the group to address it at the appropriate time.

Chapter 4

Communication

Leadership, to a large extent revolves around communication; it is the basic skill or tool around which all other facets of a leader stem. Communication comes in many forms, from the formal to the casual; the lecture to the conversation; the typed memo to the handwritten note. In this chapter we are concerned with a leader's day-to-day communication, usually spoken, with young people. It is worth noting at the very start of this chapter that formal lectures and written text, the two most common forms of communication with young people in educational situations, are notably the least effective. Written text has its place where facts must be established and confirmed, meeting times and places for example, but it is still worthwhile verbally confirming written messages to ensure they have been understood. Given the usually brief attention span of most people, let alone young people, long formal lectures should always be considered a last option for imparting information (which is obviously why our entire education system is based on them!!).

Communication (Squirrel, 1999: p25) can, amongst other things, help people to:

- share feelings
- find out things
- share information
- communicate danger or fear
- ask for things
- stop being lonely
- share ideas
- give and receive instructions

With young people the 'giving and receiving of instructions' or the 'asking for things' may be straightforward, other aspects of communication might not. One useful model to consider during communication is to think of the 'action' and 'reaction' element to each message. As an example, it would be easy to stride into a youth club and loudly and forcefully demand that the club be tidied up. The action might well be the required one, the club gets tidied, but the reaction from the young people concerned would, in all probability, be that you lose all respect and future co-operation. Another consideration is that whilst you might expect your conversations with young people to consist of meaningful and in-depth insights it is much more likely that you will encounter grunts and comments revolving around variations of 'dun know' or 's'pose so'. In addition communication with young people often has to contend with unexpected emotions and resistance. As Wheal (1998: p56) points out:

> It is arguable that adolescents, because of their unpredictable mood swings, are the most difficult people with whom to communicate successfully.

Not only do young people and 'adults' have different interests which can limit conversation they also have different styles of conversation and even, on occasions, use a 'different' language: think of text messaging as an example. Thurlow (cited in Appleyard, 2001: p16) explains how different language is used as a way of identifying belonging to a particular social or cultural grouping. Nowhere, he says, is this more evident than in adolescence:

...when the value of peer status is at a premium and as young people rework the foundations of their unique life-long project of identity construction. It is this very combination of distinguishing and bonding that makes slang and swear words an attractive linguistic resource for teenagers.

There is also a hidden message or meaning contained within much of the communication with young people, Wheal (1998: p88) gives a good example:

I didn't realise that when a young person said that it was stupid and a waste of time what they really meant was that they couldn't do it or hadn't understood. Once I realised that I was better able to cope with or avoid these difficult situations.

It is, however, usually a mistake for an adult leader to emulate the language of young people. This could lead to them becoming a figure of fun and losing the respect of the young people in their charge. In addition to the 'slang' conversation employed by young people it is also important to be aware of cultural differences in expressions used by different groups.

Young people are capable of insight and meaningful conversation but it is often up to you, the leader, to instigate it. This instigation does lead to the first rule of effective communication: all good communication is a two-way process and requires good listening skills as well as good talking skills. Listening is an active, rather than a passive skill, which requires concentration. It is also important that active prompts are used to indicate that the listener is engaging in the conversation, nodding the head, interjecting, asking questions are amongst the techniques used.

Two-way communication should be thought of as a feedback process. Listening is used to ascertain what is required, the required message is delivered and confirmed either through the receiver confirming that what they have heard is correct or the talker questioning the listener to ensure that they have understood. Questions, from either side, are used during the conversation to ensure ongoing understanding and to confirm that the message is on track and does not need to be repeated or explained.

Using prompts to keep a conversation going is an important skill: think of a doctor interviewing a patient, note how they will hold their head slightly to one side to show that they are listening and encourage the patient with nods of the head and verbal prompts (see non-verbal communication, below).

The Levels of Communication

Communication happens on a whole range of levels, much of it is less than meaningful and some of it is out and out dishonest. We are constrained to a large extent by the polite rules that society imposes on us and if we are to achieve honesty in our dealings with young people we may need to push these rules to the limit. This is because the levels of communication are to do with different levels of intimacy, depth and honesty. The ultimate example of a meaningless and dishonest conversation is one that we probably have just about every day of our lives. The routine question 'how are you?' or, more likely, 'you alright?' is almost invariably met with a response of 'fine, thanks' or, again more likely 'alright'. The conversation is a ritual cliché: we would be horrified if the respondent suddenly said 'well actually, I feel pretty awful, I had an argument with the girlfriend this morning and the dog was sick on the carpet'. This would not be playing by society's rules.

Levels of communication are shown in Figure 8 and it can be seen that ritual and cliché are only one up from complete withdrawal. As leaders we need to be able to move up the pyramid to levels where conversations are more meaningful. That is not to say that every conversation needs to be about the meaning of life, which would empty any youth club in next to no time! The 'cocktail levels' of communication are the social lubricant that keeps all conversation running.

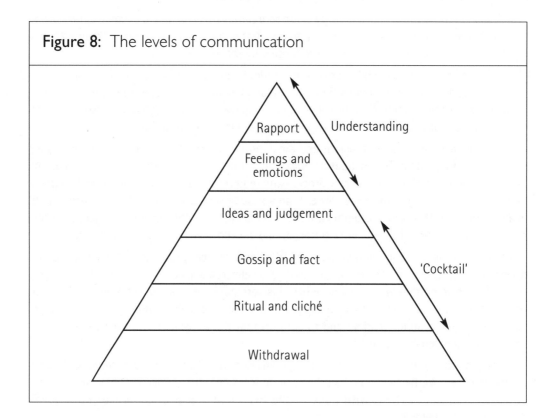

Figure 8: The levels of communication

The levels marked as 'cocktail' are essentially the components of so-called polite conversation. The most famous cliché must be the, already mentioned, expression 'how are you?' where no answer is really expected or indeed welcomed beyond a simple 'fine thanks, and you?' Ritual is best expressed in the British tradition of discussing the weather with all and sundry. Moving up the scale, 'gossip and fact' although implying a more involved conversation still does not involve the speakers on a personal level.

The same is true of 'ideas and judgements' where although opinions may be expressed the feelings behind them are not. It is not until the 'feelings and emotion' level that true communication becomes apparent with 'rapport', which is essentially non-verbal, being the ultimate in communication where true understanding is reached. The level of rapport communication is rarely reached and will, almost inevitably, involve couples of long-term standing. Married couples and established sports partners, such as in rock climbing or tennis doubles, are good examples of this.

The danger is that what may appear to be feelings and emotion can often be merely disguised ritual, for example a young person when asked how they feel about a subject will often respond with the 'acceptable' standard answer without giving any thought to it because that is the expected response. A good communicator will be able to see through this and move the conversation to higher levels.

It is important to remember, however, that when engaging in 'feelings and emotions' level dialogue people are laying themselves open in a very personal manner. This may not always be necessary and should not be forced just because of a belief that work with young people has to involve high emotions. It is often quite appropriate, for example, for a conversation to go no higher than the top end of the ideas and judgement level. Engaging in emotions is a whole different skill and needs to be approached with caution, if you open the emotional box you must be sure that you will be able to close it again: for the young person involved and for yourself (see Chapter 12 Coping with emotions).

Non-verbal Communication

It is important before you attempt any form of meaningful conversation that you are aware of the non-verbal messages that you are giving out, and the messages that are coming from others. Communication is not only about talking, the great majority of it is non-verbal. It has been suggested that as little as seven per cent of a conversation is transmitted by what is said, whilst 38 per cent is transmitted by how it is said and 55 per cent is transmitted by other non-verbal language. The cliché response mentioned above of 'alright' would immediately be seen as false if the person was in tears, but not all non-verbal communication is so obvious. It can also be open to wide misinterpretation; for example, is someone running their fingers through their hair because they are lying, a 'classic' sign, or because they have an itchy scalp? The same can also be said of your own actions; is sitting on the edge of your desk open and welcoming or patronising and intimidating? Obviously it depends on the people involved and the message you want to give, and a host of other signals. Be very careful of jumping to conclusions based on non-verbal messages.

It is also worth considering clothing as sending non-verbal signals, a collar and tie in a youth club situation usually sends a strong, possibly negative, signal of being the person in charge for example. Whilst it is important to dress appropriately for the occasion it is never worth trying to dress the same as young people. As with attempting to speak like them this would quickly lose the leader all respect the young people might have for them.

The easiest signals to interpret, and use, are the common sense ones; sitting behind a desk is an immediate barrier to communication for example. Likewise delivering an awkward message can be softened by sitting next to someone rather than standing in front of them with your hands on your hips. Being at a different height generally is a barrier to communication and is often used by overbearing managers as a way of emphasising a power relationship. Body language such as folded arms (defensive) or pursed lips (anger) all makes a difference to communication. A good indication of someone being nervous would be fidgeting with their clothing, whilst covering the mouth or bringing the hand up to the mouth is often seen as an indicator of lying.

It is important, however, that the cultural significance of some non-verbal gestures is recognised. Avoiding eye contact would be considered a sign of suspicious behaviour in most western cultures but merely politeness or deference in some Asian cultures. Likewise giggling would be considered rude in some cultures but a sign of embarrassment in others. Another culturally significant gesture is the use of personal space. In India and many other Asian countries personal space, and indeed privacy, is considered much less important than it is in the west where standing close to someone would be considered rude at best and threatening at worst.

Touch

Touch is often disregarded as a non-verbal method of communication but it is actually one of the most powerful ways of communicating there is. As Wheal (1998: p68) says:

> *Touch is the most powerful of all communication tools. Touch is the bottom line of communication...Because touch is so powerful it can work well for you if judged correctly. However, because it is so powerful it can seriously damage your relationship with anyone if you get it wrong.*

This is the dilemma of using touch; a consoling hug can be the perfect thing at a moment of crisis or it could cause a complete misunderstanding. Some professions, such as teaching, now consider that all touch is inappropriate because we live in a society where even the slightest action can be misconstrued (see Chapter 12 Allegations of abuse). However, if a leader knows the young people they are working with and, more importantly, they respect them and there are clear boundaries, touch is such a valuable tool that it cannot be neglected. Even a simple hand on someone's shoulder can convey caring, be a calming gesture or indicate solidarity. If in doubt stick to safe, conventional gestures such as a hand on the shoulder or even hand shaking until boundaries are established.

Tonal communication

Allied to non-verbal communication is the tone of a conversation, sometimes referred to as paralanguage, and how things are said, Graham (1997: p89) gives us this example:

> *Andy, a pleasant if somewhat clumsy fellow doesn't realise he's slowing up the entire group (whilst walking). When he catches up at one point, he gulps his breath and then asks you, 'How'm I doing?'*
>
> *You can:*
> - *Understand that he's doing his best, and to encourage him, smile and reply with a cheery 'you're doing just fine';*
> - *Resign yourself to his incompetence and mumble, 'you're doing just fine' in a low monotone, almost under your breath;*
> - *Seethe with anger and turn on him with a cynical 'you're doing just fine.'*
>
> *The words are the same. The messages are totally different.*

Obviously one of the problems with tonal and non-verbal communication is that it can convey messages that have to do with how you are feeling and which may have nothing to do with the situation at hand. If you have just come straight from an argument with one person, for example, you will probably be giving off aggressive or defensive signals such as tight lips, crossed arms, low voice and so on. The next young person you talk to could interpret these gestures at being aimed at them and mistakenly think that it is them that you are angry at, even though you think you spoke to them in a cordial and polite manner. All leaders, but especially leaders working with young people, need to learn how to compartmentalise their feelings and emotions so that one situation doesn't spill out into another (see Chapter 12 Looking After Yourself and Others).

Obviously it is important to avoid misunderstandings, which is where two-way communication comes in, but it is also important to avoid turning a conversation into a defensive situation; intentionally or otherwise. The energy in any conversation that is perceived by either party as being aggressive or containing accusations is directed towards self-defence rather than resolution. This can lead to a downward spiral where all future communication is received in a defensive manner and this attitude can affect others amongst the peer group. Defensive behaviour is also aroused in the initial communicator who is keen to defend what they perceive as their original meaning. All communication then becomes distorted through a self-defence filter that renders the true meaning and value of the communication as meaningless. Wheal (1998: p62) highlights the following pairs of categories as indicators of defensive, or supportive, communication:

Defensive	–	Supportive
Evaluation	–	Descriptive
Control	–	Problem orientation
Strategy	–	Spontaneity
Neutrality	–	Empathy
Superiority	–	Equality
Closed mind	–	Open mind

Any communication that contains elements from the left hand column may arouse defensive behaviour whilst elements from the right hand column will indicate supportive behaviour. Obviously the amount of defensive behaviour exhibited by the receiver can also be an indicator of other circumstances and situations that may be completely outside of the control of the communicator. In this instance it is even more important that the communicator utilises as many of the supportive elements as possible. In particular it is important that the communicator is perceived as open, empathetic and honest.

Effective Communication: Some Golden Rules

The features of effective communication (B.T., 1997) can be neatly summarised as:
- It is a genuine two-way experience.
- Both sides are heard and understood with both sides being open.
- The atmosphere is comfortable enabling important things to be said.
- The conversation or communication makes a difference.

A lot of conversation fails to achieve its objective and results in misunderstanding. The following pointers are essential for establishing effective communication:
- Always think clearly before you start talking: engage brain before opening mouth! Know what you are going to say and the objective of the conversation. Clarify in your own mind what it is that you want to communicate and confirm the most effective way of putting it across.

- Consider the timing of the conversation and the climate in which it is to take place, for example bringing up a person's failings when they are in floods of tears may well not be appropriate!
- How you say something can be as important as what you say. Consider the overtones of the conversation. Ask yourself how the recipient feels, try to put yourself in their shoes.
- Be aware of body language and your physical position.
- Be aware that communication involves people and that language is simply one of many mediums that can be used.

Getting People to Talk: *Activities*

Many of these activities have their basis in counselling and you should be aware, or even beware, that they can open flood gates (see Chapter 12 Coping with emotions).

Getting started

Start with some simple games, physical ones are usually best (see also the activities at the end of Chapter 6) as they distract the students away from the hidden agenda: getting a conversation going. The formal introduction where people introduce themselves or their 'partners' usually seems awkward and self-defeating.

Circular names. A fun way to get people introducing themselves and helping others in the group to remember names. Get the group to stand in a circle and using a beanbag or something similar get them to throw the bag to each other. On the first round they simply say their name and then as the name progresses they say their name and something about themselves, build up to students talking about the person they are throwing the bag to. *(Be aware that some students will still find this awkward if they have a poor memory for names: try and get the students to say memorable things, silly is usually best!)*

Common crossword. An alternative, or addition, to circular names that encourages people to talk to each other. Members of the group need to introduce themselves to each other and find something that they have in common. This then needs to be written, with their names on a strip of paper and pinned on a large board. As the board fills up with strips of paper other members of the group can add their names to the strips, but only if they find another person with the same thing in common. The imagination can then run riot with strips being connected to others by name and commonality.

Walking the plank. Use a plank raised a few centimetres of the ground, on bricks for example, with the group lined up on the plank, and not allowed to get off, get them to put themselves in order of height, age or anything else you can think of. Try it without anyone speaking. This also gets them used to contact with each other, which is a useful way of breaking down barriers. *(Be aware: physical contact is not always welcome amongst teenagers, be ready to set some ground rules about behaviour or allow people to opt out if you have to.)*

Ultimate non-verbal communication. Challenge your group to express emotions without speaking, i.e. using body language only, if they are too good challenge them to do it using nothing but facial expressions.

In deeper

If you are challenging people, some would say confronting, where emotions are raised you should always set some ground rules, or even better get your students to set them. Examples would be; everybody is listened to with respect, everything said is confidential, anyone can opt out if they feel the need to etc. (see Chapter 9 Reviewing and Feedback).

One good way of getting young people to talk about personal issues is for them to draw, for example drawing a tree that represents their life, and then explain to the group why they have drawn what they have. This can be a very powerful tool but it is important that no one tries to read anything into the drawings other than what the young person is willing to discuss; the point of the exercise is to get people talking not to psychoanalyse their drawings.

Two-way communication

A good exercise to demonstrate the importance of two-way communication is to ask a group member to describe a complicated shape to their group. This should be done with no physical help, tell them to put their hands behind their back, and no questioning from the group. Next get them to describe another shape but this time the group can ask questions, this will, usually, be much more effective. This exercise also demonstrates how much we tend to use our hands in normal conversation.

The importance of clear communication

The object of the exercise is, with the entire group blindfolded, to make a complete, preferably large, square with a piece of rope or cord. This exercise will make it very clear how relying on speech only is not a very effective way of communicating but, when it is all that is allowed, the communication must be very clear.

Chapter 5

Motivating Young People

Sometimes one of the most frustrating aspects to leadership with young people can be in getting them motivated. This is a huge subject and what is presented here is, of necessity, merely an introduction.

An Introduction to Motivation

Although the study of motivation is a complex and sometimes bewildering subject, motivation itself can be simply described. This exact definition of motivation is one that has taken various forms as the science of psychology has progressed. The term 'motivation' itself has evolved from the Latin *movere*, meaning 'to move'. In a sense motivation can be regarded as the force required to move, or drive, a person to take a particular action.

It is generally accepted, however, that motivation consists of more than just a simple drive. We now say that motivation is made up of three separate components which are referred to as *the motivation construct* (Steers and Porter, 1991) This consists of:

- How the behaviour is directed: the drive, or direction, component.
- How the behaviour is energised: the vigour component.
- How the behaviour is sustained: the persistence component.

These mean, when working with young people, that motivation needs to be thought of in three parts: what do you want the young people to do, how do you get them excited about it and how do you keep them going. Before this stage is reached, however, it is important to understand the two 'schools' of motivation, those which deal with needs and those which deal with methods.

The former, which deal with needs, is commonly referred to as the '*humanist*' school; this category is often seen as being exemplified by the eminent psychologist Carl Rogers (1902–1987). A central belief of this school is that the most important determinants of human behaviour are inner qualities, notably a will to grow and develop towards fulfilment.

The second school of theory is one which deals with the processes used to encourage motivation and for this reason is often referred to as 'process theory' or the '*behaviourist*' school. This category of theory starts from the assumption that people can be motivated by extrinsic means, pay and reward being the classic examples. Much of process theory has been influenced by the work of Ivan Pavlov (1849–1936) who showed that dogs could be made to salivate at a neutral stimulus which had been associated with food. This response, known as 'a conditioned response' has generally become known as the basis of the 'carrot and stick' type of motivation.

The difference between the two schools, and what makes them important to leaders, is that the first, humanist approach, maintains that people are self-motivating, given the right conditions, whilst the second, behaviourist approach, maintains that people need external motivation; the carrot and stick. Unfortunately we live in a society that tends to believe in the humanist approach but actually uses the behaviourist approach. This means that as a leader of young people you may well be dealing with people who are used to either being rewarded for doing something or punished for not doing it. As has been discussed elsewhere in this book, 'carrot and stick' motivation may bring about the required action but rarely the required reaction. A major problem is that when the carrot and stick is removed then the extrinsic motivation also goes. It has also been shown that motivating people through rewards or punishment is rarely effective for more than the short term. It is internal, self-motivating, behaviour that needs to be encouraged to achieve long-term benefit. However, because of what young people may have become accustomed to, attempting to appeal to their 'better nature' can be an up-hill struggle in the first instance. The key to winning this up-hill struggle lies in probably the most famous theory of motivation of them all; Maslow's Hierarchy.

Maslow's Hierarchy of Needs

Perhaps because of its simple and elegant nature, one of the most popular motivation theories in use today is Maslow's Hierarchy of Needs (1943). This theory says that people have several layers of needs that have to be fulfilled starting with basic physical needs and moving up, through safety, social and esteem needs, to needs of growth and self-actualisation. It is only when each level of need is satisfied that the person can become motivated to satisfy the needs of the next level. Self-actualisation is seen as the ultimate goal of a person who on reaching it becomes 'fully-functioning' in harmony with their own needs and feelings and at one with others. Maslow's classical model (Figure 9) is the ascending pyramid.

In terms of our everyday life the lower two needs, physiological and safety, can be equated to such physical things as food, shelter, clothing and 'law and order'. These tend to be relatively easy to satisfy for the majority of people, although safety needs do depend on having a reliable and structured home background for fulfilment. In an age where an increasing number of young people have two 'sets' of family through divorced parents this needs to be taken into account.

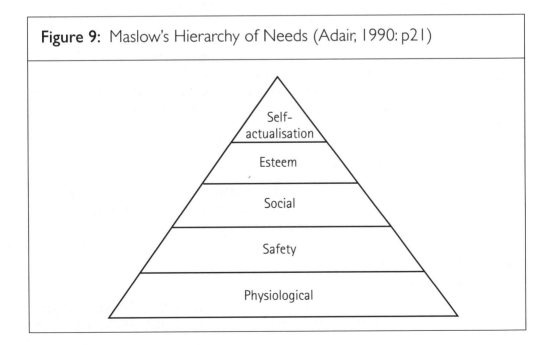

Figure 9: Maslow's Hierarchy of Needs (Adair, 1990: p21)

The next two levels, of social and esteem needs, are rather more difficult, particularly in today's society with its emphasis on competition and predominantly selfish behaviour. Traditionally social needs have been met through the family and friends whilst esteem needs have been met through peer recognition and internal confidence. It is within the environment that can be established through youth organisations and clubs plus the support and respect of peers that leaders can have the biggest impact on these needs. It is, however, important that esteem needs are met by genuine approval and acceptance and in addition the self-esteem must be fulfilled. It is the fulfilment of this need that generates self-confidence.

Self-actualisation can be seen as the ultimate, and realistically unlikely, goal of self-development where a person reaches their full potential. Maslow (cited in Adair, 1990: p38) wrote of self-actualisation that:

> Even if all (the first four) needs are satisfied, we may still often, if not always, expect that a new discontent and restlessness will soon develop, unless the individual is doing what he is fitted for. A musician must make music, an artist must paint, a poet must write, if he is to be ultimately at peace with himself. What a man can be, he must be. This need we may call self-actualisation.

The important aspect of Maslow's Hierarchy is that it maintains that all people are driven to improve themselves and ultimately reach the goal of self-actualisation, however this can only be done if the lower needs are satisfied. As leaders of young people it can be seen that if we want to apply this theory of motivation we need to ensure that the lower needs are satisfied. Much of this comes down to the way we work with, and respect as individuals, the young people in our charge. It has been said that the most important thing that a leader of young people can do is to give them a high, genuine, level of self-esteem which in turn will give them the confidence to take risks with their lives in search of fulfilment. Maslow's theory would seem to support this suggestion. However, on the down side, Maslow's theory would also suggest that those young people who do not have their lower level needs met, through a broken home, deprivation etc., will be unable to move up through the levels. As it would be unusual for the leader of young people to be able to influence these lower level needs this could present a significant barrier when encouraging young people to become self-fulfilling. This does make a great deal of sense, if a young person is constantly hungry or deprived of human affection it is unlikely that they will be looking to satisfy higher order needs. In such a situation the leader involved will probably have to look to external agencies for help in satisfying the young person's needs (see Chapter 12 Looking After Yourself and Others).

Achievement Theories

There are two main theories which look at peoples motivation to succeed, these are achievement motivation theory and attribution theory. Achievement motivation theory, which was developed by McClelland (1961) says that people have three main needs:

- the need for achievement
- the need for affiliation
- the need for power

McClelland argued that everyone has all of these needs but to highly varying greater or lesser extents. People with a high need for achievement may display a tendency for success due to realistic goal setting but they are not noted as being good team members because of their need to exercise responsibility. The aspect of goal setting is a critical area of achievement theory and stipulates that whilst high need achievers will set realistic goals, low need achievers will set goals that are either too high or too low. This allows them to have either an excuse for failure or an excuse for easy success. Having obtained easy success the person with low achievement needs has no need to increase the level of future goals, thus avoiding the possibility of failure.

People who exhibit high affiliation needs are noted as good team workers who regard the social aspects of the workplace as highly important. In successful people however this need will rarely be dominant.

The need for power has been said to be the aim of all human activity. Whether this is true or not it is more certain that the need for power is the basis of leadership success. McClelland argued that there are two distinct variations of the need for power. Personal power is that where individuals exercise power for its own sake whereas social power is that where individuals are more concerned to exercise power in order to achieve the goals of an organisation or help others. Leaders who exercise a high need for power by itself can be counter-productive in their relationships with others. However, if combined with other needs, and in particular achievement needs, it can lead to highly productive results.

The main premise of attribution theory is that an individual needs to feel (attribute) that achieving a set goal was largely due to their efforts. Figure 10, which illustrates this, makes it quite clear that attribution is biased (thicker arrow) in the direction of internal attribution.

Likewise, according to this theory people aim for success by carrying out tasks which they know are within their capabilities although for real feelings of success the activity needs to contain a suitable degree of challenge.

Rotter's (1954, cited in Weiner, 1974) locus of control theory showed that the attributions highlighted in Figure 10 could be stable or unstable. Figure 11, which combines the elements of

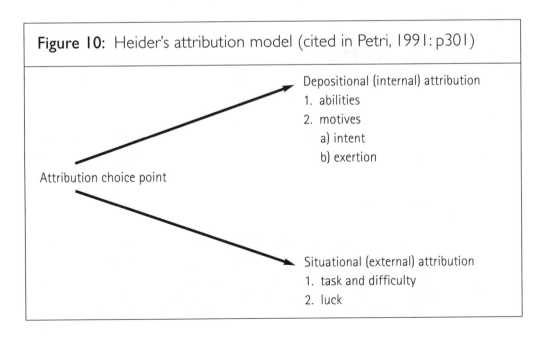

Figure 10: Heider's attribution model (cited in Petri, 1991: p301)

Attribution choice point

Depositional (internal) attribution
1. abilities
2. motives
   a) intent
   b) exertion

Situational (external) attribution
1. task and difficulty
2. luck

stability and instability with internal and external attributions, is the widely seen model found in general use today.

The attribution model highlights the way in which success at a task is attributed by a person to internal and external factors, locus of control, and relates that to the expectancy, stability dimensions, of repeating that success. It can be seen, for example, that success gained through ability is a constant dimension and therefore engenders a high probability of being repeated. However, if the external factor of difficulty is not right, for example it is too low and the task is accomplished easily, there will be no associated feeling of pride.

Figure 11: Attribution theory model (adapted from Weiner, 1974)

| | | Attribution | |
		Internal	External
Stability	**Stable**	Ability	Task difficulty
	Unstable	Effort	Luck

The opposite of this is that if the task level is set at a very high level success may be attributed to luck. This being an unstable dimension, there will be a low expectancy of future success. In a similar manner failure can also be associated with stable and unstable dimensions. Failure attributed to a perceived feeling of low effort being put into a task will, for example, possibly lead the person to believe that success is attainable in the future. Failure due to the task being too hard or through lack of ability, both stable dimensions, will lead the person to expect failure in future efforts.

What Does it all Mean?

Motivation theory, unfortunately, does not do such a great job of telling us how to motivate young people but it is a valuable aid in helping us to understand what motivates them. As Handy (1993: p53) says:

> *Having got this far in an overview of motivation the reader may perhaps be experiencing, as I did, a sense of disappointment...I had hoped that motivation theories would reveal to me the true purpose of my life and my raison d'être...From this position of disappointment I came to recognise that motivation theory is useful as a way of understanding how most individuals, given who they are, go about making the short and medium term decisions in their life.*

Thus, achievement theory is well worth studying because if a leader working with young people understands what is driving them, they will be in a better position to harness that motivation. For example, if it is obvious that someone has a high level of affiliation needs then their role in the peer group environment will be important whereas someone who has high achievement needs will need to be focused on tasks that reward that need. This then needs to be balanced against attribution theory; which is an excellent way to investigate how young people lay the blame and responsibility on other forces or accept it for themselves. Maslow's Hierarchy meanwhile gives a good synopsis of the forces that act on all of us to achieve something worthwhile in our lives. Incidentally, Maslow's Hierarchy goes a long way to explaining the high standards and drive that can push many leaders into a situation of exhaustion and burnout (see Chapter 12 Burnout). There is an innate sense of altruism and vocationalism in much of the work of a leader dealing with young people that has many similarities to the drive to self-actualisation.

One thing that is certain is that young people do often have an acute sense of fairness that can play a big part in their motivation. Equity theory is often seen as the principle theory when discussing fairness. One of the main attractions of this theory is that it has a firm 'common sense' basis which makes it easily understood by the layman. The basic assumption of equity theory is that people seek fairness, or justice, in their relationships such as those in their dealings with adults. Perceived imbalances in this relationship, i.e. unfairness, are assumed to result in tension that causes them to find ways of redressing this imbalance, usually be misbehaving in some way. Developing this feeling of equity people will balance the ratio of a persons inputs and outcomes against the equivalent ratio of the other person involved in the exchange or against a third person involved in a similar exchange. Again the person concerned will be looking to see if that ratio is similar, in other words they are getting the same reward for the same effort. It is important, therefore that the treatment of young people is not only fair but seen to be fair when measured against the treatment of other people. It is, of course, the very fact that a modern society is not 'fair' that causes many of the problems with young people in such areas as crime and delinquency. The work of a young leader is to demonstrate that as much fairness as possible *in the given situation* is being applied. Sometimes young people simply have to be told that they can't have everything they want purely on the grounds of 'fairness'.

An important aspect when considering the motivation of young people is empowerment. As a rule they will be much more likely to engage with a task or exercise if they have had some say over what it involves. Wilson (1995: p280) makes the point that:

> *...providing that space for individuals or groups to set their own goals is one of the most important keys to making the event empowering. It sets into motion that vehicle for intrinsic motivation that really lets the experience belong to the learner.*

It can often surprise even the most experienced of leaders working with young people that what the leader thinks is a good idea can have little connection with what the young people themselves think. It is worth perhaps considering that transplanting an adult's motivations and interests onto a young person will ultimately be futile or even counter-productive. At best we can empathise with a young person's motivation and at least we can attempt to understand the reasoning behind it.

Finally Adair (1990: pp94–101) gives some pertinent tips for motivating people:

Be motivated yourself

> *The first and golden rule of motivation is that you will never inspire others unless you are inspired yourself. Only a motivated leader motivates others.*

Treat each person as an individual

Unless you ask a person what motivates them, what they want, you will not know. For we are all individuals. What motivates one person in the team may not motivate another. Enter into some sort of dialogue with each individual.

Set realistic and challenging targets

There is a fine balance here. If objectives are totally unrealistic they will demotivate people; if they are too easy to attain, on the other hand, they are also uninspiring. As a leader you have to get the balance right.

Remember that progress motivates

It is a sound principle that progress motivates. If people know they are moving forward it leads them to increase their efforts. We invest more in success.

Create a motivating environment

Although you have limited power to motivate others you can do a great deal to create an environment which they will find motivating...check that people do have proper input into the decisions that affect their working lives.

Provide fair rewards

Fairness or justice means that the return should be equivalent in value to the contribution.

Give recognition

This thirst for recognition is universal...as a leader you can give recognition and show appreciation in a variety of ways. A sincere 'well done' or 'thank you' can work wonders for a person's morale...but it is equally important to encourage a climate where each person recognises the worth or value of the contribution of others...for it is recognition by our peers, discerning equals or colleagues, that we value even more than the praise of superiors.

Chapter 6

Teamwork

It is not uncommon for the leader of young people to be primarily focused on team or group spirit. Whilst individuals and the task at hand (see Chapter 3 Action centred leadership) are both important considerations, the practicalities of much of a leader's work revolve around groups of people. In addition so-called 'personal development' programmes and courses often have a group work, rather than an individual, basis. This chapter looks at the characteristics of effective teams and the roles played within teams. It then looks at team development, the stages that teams go through and the barriers to that development. The chapter concludes by looking at how to maintain the team.

The development of teams in a course situation can range from the simple 'bonding' weekend where a group of colleagues get together for a weekend of activities ranging from rock climbing to driving battle tanks in order to get to know each other better, to the other extreme of very serious courses designed to address specific issues. The leader of young people will, however, often be concerned with the long-term development of a group of people such as in a Duke of Edinburgh's Award or youth team scenario. The primary issues remain the same whether the development is course based or long term. They almost inevitably include:

- Communication—inter personal and inter team or group.
- Trust—between peers and between seniors and juniors.
- Responsibilities—their acceptance and division.
- Reward and praise—and criticism.

It is important to recognise that in early team sessions many issues, especially communication and trust, will be put forward by a group as the expected cliché answers. It will take some time to get beyond this initial stage (see Chapter 4 Communication and Chapter 13 Measuring Success).

Characteristics of Effective Teams

Bad teamwork is often characterised by an increase in bureaucracy usually with long winded procedures, chains of command and autocratic leadership. A result of this is that personal territories and tasks are vigorously defended with accompanying feuds between teams, sub-groups within teams, individuals within teams and leaders and teams. The ultimate result of all this is a poor concentration on whatever the objective happens to be with repeated and duplicated tasks caused by lack of co-operation and a poor, even hostile, working environment. This misplaced use of energy in a bad team is demonstrated by the team climate model of Vincent Nolan (1987) shown in Figure 12. This shows that, in a threatening or adversarial team, energy is wasted on emotional survival rather than completing the task.

Team size has a significant effect on both team development and function. In an ideal world teams would be kept small enough to maintain close working links with effective, and open, communication but large enough to provide support and task effectiveness. In reality this will almost always end up as a compromise situation. What does seem certain is that teams that contain more than five or six members need to develop a more hierarchical system, with structured leadership, in order to be effective. It can be argued that the larger team which functions in

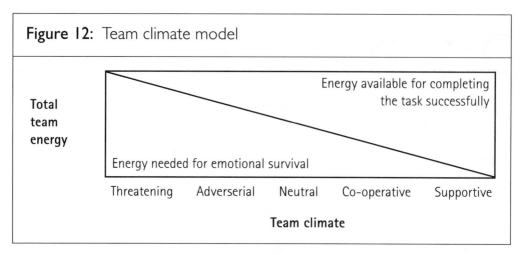

Figure 12: Team climate model

Total team energy

Energy available for completing the task successfully

Energy needed for emotional survival

Threatening   Adverserial   Neutral   Co-operative   Supportive

Team climate

total harmony by virtue of concord without the need for leadership is a myth. A debatable point, perhaps, but always a good one to put into a group discussion!

There are many lists of the features that constitute an effective team. The list below, presented in no particular order, is a composite of the common features typically found on these lists:

- A clear and commonly shared vision of the purpose and aims of the team.
- Good communication within the team and with other teams, this includes good listening skills.
- Openness when confronting difficult issues and the support needed to make this possible.
- Consensus rather than compromise in decision making.
- Appropriate level of leadership together with support for the leadership and effective delegation of responsibilities.
- A willingness to confront traditional working practices.
- A willingness to accept help, both from within and without the team together with high levels of co-operation.
- High levels of mutual trust especially across the various levels of seniority.
- Constant development of the team and individuals within it.
- Regular reviews of technical and personnel/personal issues.
- A willingness to use creative conflict, rather than aimless and destructive competition.
- Efficient and commonly agreed decision making procedures and working practices.
- The ability to adapt to change, including accepting new team members.
- And finally, useful meetings rather than endless talking in circles!

Team Roles

If there is one psychological test/computer programme which is used more than any other on team building development it is probably that developed by Meredith Belbin (1983). As with many of these models it is perhaps more widely used than understood. In essence, through a series of tick box questions, it identifies a number of team roles that Belbin maintains are needed to build an effective team. These roles are shown in Figure 13. The Belbin test is typically done by the individual, in other words the results are how a person sees themselves, it can be done with people ticking the boxes for their fellow team members but this is unusual and may be problematic.

What is often missed by many of those using the Belbin model, and test, is that the roles identified are volatile; in other words they are not fixed. This is an important point because all too often students on courses are told they are, for example, predominately a 'resource investigator' and led to believe that this is their fixed personality. This is not the case; a person's role can change through such developments as education, experience, promotion, maturity and so on. In addition to this all people will play a number of different roles to a greater or lesser degree and few people will be characterised by one or two roles at the expense of all the others.

Although Belbin has become almost an industry standard, the awkward terms he uses to describe some of the team roles means that simpler terms are often used instead. These can be purely task oriented roles, for example co-ordinator, time-keeper, record keeper and so on or they can reflect Belbin's ideas using such terms as thinker, worker, leader and resource controller. Likewise negative terms can be applied to such people as the shirker, criticiser, dominator or troublemaker. The difficulty with many of these terms is in the application. Using anonymous cards can be one technique to label team members after an exercise but whilst this may protect those doing the describing, the feelings of those being described can still be badly hurt. One of the joys of the Belbin test is that no one else need be involved.

Having said this, one of the most useful ways to identify team roles when working with a group of young people is to get them to identify firstly what team roles are needed to complete a task and secondly what roles team members actually fulfilled during the task. These terms will probably have far more relevance to young people than any industry or team development model terms.

The Stages of Team Development

Perhaps the most popular model of team development in use today is that developed by Tuckerman and Jensen (1977) which maintains that teams go through four notable stages of Forming, Storming, Norming and Performing as shown in Figure 14.

One of the most important things to remember with the four stage model is that the stages are volatile in both directions: it is just as possible to slip backwards as it is to go forwards. This change is usually most apparent when team members, especially senior members, or the task changes. In reality few teams function for more than a short time in the performing stage. It is more likely that established teams will operate for the majority of time in the norming stage with occasional short moves towards the stages above and below that.

Some models place another stage, that of re-forming, between norming and performing. This stage allows for the issues raised during the other stages to be addressed, or re-addressed, before the team can function effectively.

Adjourning

A fifth stage, adjourning, was added by Tuckerman and Jensen to allow for the ending of the task and the dissolution of the relationships within the team. It could be argued that this is not, strictly speaking, a stage in team development, which is why the four stage model is more commonly used. However, it is important to consider when working with a group of young people, who may only be together for a finite time, how the break-up of their group will affect

Figure 13: Belbin's team roles

	Characteristics	Contribution	Weaknesses
Plant	Creative Imaginative Unorthodox	Solves difficult problems	Ignore incidentals Preoccupied Poor communicator
Resource investigator	Extrovert Enthusiastic Communicative	Explores opportunities Develops contacts	Over-optimistic Loses interest easily
Co-ordinator	Mature Confident	Clarifies goals Promotes decision making Good at delegating	Offloads own work Can be taken as manipulative
Shaper	Challenging Dynamic Works well under pressure	Overcomes obstacles Pushes ideas through	Easily provoked Can offend other people
Monitor evaluator	Sober Discerning	Sees strategic picture Sees all options Good judge of options	Fails to inspire others Can be seen to lack drive
Team worker	Co-operative Mild personality Perceptive and diplomatic	Builds team Averts friction A good listener	Indecisive under pressure
Implementer	Disciplined Reliable and efficient	Turns ideas into actions	Inflexible Conservative Slow to respond
Completer	Painstaking Conscientious	Delivers on time Searches out errors and mistakes	Inclined to worry Bad at delegating
Specialist	Dedicated Single-minded Self-sufficient	Provides specialist knowledge and skills	Dwells on technical issues Only contributes on technical points

individuals. Although the outward signs of the adjourning process are usually negative, crying, missing friendships etc. it should not be thought that the process is entirely negative. Allison (2000: p34) likens the process to grieving but comments that:

Rather than being negative it appears that it is actually an indication of personal growth and adjustment, even though it can be difficult. If there were no signs of some form of (adjournment) adjustment then one could question if there had been any changes or examination of values during the...experience.

Figure 14: The stages of team development	
Forming (immature team or ritual sniffing) sometimes termed undeveloped team	• Considerable anxiety. • Testing to discover the nature of the group. • The leader is looked to for decisions. • Low levels of productivity. • Questions are asked about what is appropriate behaviour. • Communication is at a polite level. • Expectations are raised about the future. The team needs structure, leadership and standards.
Storming (fractionated team) sometimes termed experimenting team	• Opinions become polarised. • Authority in the leader is questioned and challenged. • Communication is characterised by argument. • There is a dip in morale and disillusionment with expectations. • Team members jostle for superiority and clear roles. The team needs resolution of conflicts and agreement regarding tasks and team roles.
Norming (sharing team) sometimes termed consolidating team	• The team becomes comfortable and possibly complacent. • Communication is based around an open exchange of ideas. • There is support and co-operation amongst team members. • Plans and standards are agreed. • Team members are careful not to upset others in order to avoid a return to the storming stage. • Productivity is reasonable but not high or effective. The team needs greater interdependence and task focus together with the confidence to face up to conflict issues.
Performing (effective team) sometimes termed mature team	• Team energy is applied to the task rather than personnel issues. • There are feelings of pride and eagerness. • Team members are capable of both interdependent and independent action. • The team is clearly structured in an appropriate manner. • Roles are defined and yet remain flexible. The team needs an awareness of itself in order not to slip back into the norming stage.

Given this, it is an important element of the adjourning process to clarify and rationalise what has been the value of the task or experience that is coming to an end and what has been the learning or development gained from it. Even more critically, perhaps, it is important to foster discussion or reflection on how that learning can be carried over into whatever is coming next for the young people involved. Adjourning can be a difficult time for a leader who is often already thinking about the next group or the next task. It should, however, be given the respect that it warrants, particularly if it is a vital transitory moment as will often be the case when young people are involved.

In many cases it is worthwhile to consider follow-up strategies that might come some time after a programme where strong feelings or emotions were engendered. It is often the case that some time after a programme or experience the young people involved need to contact others in their group, or the leader, to talk through feelings which have arisen since the experience or to make sense of what was learnt. These cannot be dealt with at the end of the experience or programme because they may take time to be assimilated, emotions may be too strong at that time or the young person needs a significant break away from the group to reflect on what has happened. It is also frequently the case that after returning to their home environment a young person struggles to put their learning or development into context away from where it happened. The benefits of an intense learning experience can easily, and all too frequently are, lost in this way. It is down to the leader to ensure that support is available to the young people in their charge after they have moved on. This may be as simple as encouraging a group to exchange addresses, e-mails and phone numbers or it may necessitate arranging to bring the group back together again in the future. This continuing contact is where the leader who has an ongoing relationship with 'their' group of young people has the advantage over the leader who only sees them for a short finite, but often very intense, period of time. In either case, however, the leader needs to ensure that young people are not left to cope by themselves after an emotional experience (but see Chapter 12 Burnout).

Barriers to Team Development

A badly developed team is more than just the opposite of a good team; there are additional barriers that may act to prevent the development of teams. A leader working with young people will come across many of these barriers on both team development courses and long-term team development. Issues such as these will usually need to be addressed through review and discussion. Occasionally it may be necessary to take more direct techniques such as 'gagging' key team members to allow the team as a whole to develop.

There is a knowledge gap within the team

In simple, and simplistic, terms this is often manifested on courses by the ex-scout phenomenon. This is where the ex-scouts tie all the knots and build the raft whilst the non ex-scouts feel intimidated by the seemingly knowledgeable activity being undertaken and therefore decline to play any role other than observer. There can also be much deeper different levels of people, thinking and communication skills that need to be overcome.

Sub-groups exist within the team

Again, in simplistic terms, this can be as simple as all the smokers sticking together because they are forced to take their breaks outside of the review room. Almost any sub-group will tend to be counter-productive.

There is rivalry between team members

It has been known for career prospects or even future employment to depend on performance on a course. This is, however, highly destructive and thankfully rare. Rivalry and power politics are only natural amongst any group of people and can result in healthy competition as well as disruption.

There are underlying tensions within the team

These can be particularly difficult to handle because the leader may be totally unaware of their cause and sometimes even their very existence. Clues such as a blatant reluctance of two people to work together may indicate a history of conflict that will need to be resolved, preferably by the people involved.

The myth of 'the super team'

This is where a team believes, or is led to believe, that it is some kind of super team. Managers' pep talks are a good example of this where underlying problems are swept aside by a deluge of rhetoric leaving the team unable to face its real difficulties.

There is unrealistic bonding

Similar to the myth of the super team is where the team has bonded to an unhealthy, and unhelpful degree leaving people unable to express true feelings, particularly about each other, for fear of upsetting the team spirit. This is often seen where the team is asked to rate each other's performance and each team member is given the same score.

In addition to these if the team is taken out of its normal situation its members are likely to maintain their normal roles even if these are not appropriate. An example of this might be where a youth football team relies on its coach to make decisions even in a non-football situation. This is obviously counter-productive as it stifles more effective team roles being established.

Maintenance and Needs of the Team

And finally, an effective team will have a number of needs in order to continue operating. The needs below are based on the list identified by John Jones (1973) and consist of:

The need for diversity

A team is made up of individuals. Not only will each individual have weak points they will also have strengths and skills. For a team to operate at maximum effectiveness these individual strong points need to be not only encouraged and utilised but also as diverse as possible in order to give depth and breadth to the team.

The need for safety

Fear and suspicion can come from both within and without the team; both are a barrier to effective operation. The team needs to provide a safe environment from which to accept and face challenges. This can only be done if trust, respect and openness exist between team members.

The need for shared commitment

A team is not only about individual motivation but also, and more importantly, about a shared aim, purpose and vision. A shared commitment and strength of purpose will be needed most when the end goal of a task becomes lost or blurred. Without the shared commitment of a successful team individuals will go their own way and conflict will arise when difficulties arise.

The need for team identity

A strong team identity reflects the need, within the majority of people, for belonging. Team identity is reflected in integrity and perseverance to maintain standards in the face of difficulties. Team members need to be proud of their team and have not only a sense of belonging but also a sense of shared ownership.

The need for trust

A key feature of an effective team is that the individuals within the team feel they can rely on each other. This trust needs to be developed and built on through openness and honesty and carefully preserved. A team that loses trust in each other will be difficult to bring back together again.

The need for continuous development

Just as individuals so too do teams need to develop and change. A team must be prepared to take new risks, accept new truths, roles and agendas or it will stagnate, become inflexible and, eventually, redundant.

In addition to these needs the 'perfect team' will still need maintenance in order to keep it that way. This can be done in a number of ways, notably though:

- Encouraging—giving praise and reassurance.
- Harmonising—resolving disputes and the easing of conflict.
- Gate-keeping—making sure all team members have a role.
- Standard setting—setting rules of conduct and behaviour.
- Following—actively going along with team strategy.

Team Building and Bonding: *Activities*

There are many team building exercises available ranging from the very simple lasting a few minutes to the very complex lasting days or even weeks. These are just a few suggestions that are quick and easy and require a minimum of equipment. Many of these exercises are interchangeable with the communication exercises at the end of Chapter 4. As with all exercises think about simple safety precautions such as removing high heels and jewellery and ensuring things do not get too far out of hand. It is usually worth setting a few ground rules at the beginning of a session.

Circle run-around. This game is basically a bit of fun to get people moving. The group stands in a circle facing inwards. One nominated person stands in the middle of the circle and shouts a characteristic that one or more of the group may have. E.g. All those with blue eyes, or all those wearing blue socks etc. All those that qualify have to swap places with another person that has the characteristic (across the centre of the circle). The person in the middle has to get into one of the available spare places before anyone else. The characteristics can get preferably as silly as possible! The person left without a place shouts the next characteristic.

Paddle race. This game will add an element of competition and introduce teamwork. Split the group into smaller groups, it helps to have at least three per group. Get the groups to sit down in a line, one person behind the other. The front person has a paddle, (pole or broom) which they must pass back by leaning back and passing the paddle over their head to the person behind. Once they have passed the paddle they must then run to the back of the line, ready to receive the paddle. The aim is to get from point A to point B before the other groups.

Skin the snake. A good way for people to get to know each other! The group stands in a line one behind the other, each person reaches through their legs with one hand and with the other hand holds the hand of the person in front of them. The front person in the group, followed by everyone in turn, has to then walk backwards over the entire group. The end result should be the whole group standing in the opposite order still holding hands. See if they can reverse the process!

Noah's ark. A great game to release any inhibitions and bring the group onto an even footing (i.e. everyone feels silly!). Each person in the group is given an animal to be. Within the group there must be two of each animal chosen. When you give the signal everyone has to find their partner and make their way to a given point known as the ark. However! they can only make the noise and physical action associated with their given animal.

Sit down circle. This game is a good settling/relaxing game and encourages teamwork. It can break down barriers. The group stands in a circle and each member turns 90 degrees to the right (with youngsters – get them to put up their right hand to ensure they all turn the correct way!). Everyone should now be looking at someone's back! Get the group to take a number of steps to the left so they are close together. The object of the game is to get everyone sitting on the knee of the person behind them. Leave it up to the group to organise or direct the group exactly. Once they are all sat down see if the whole circle can walk forward!

Human monster. One way to get the whole group moving together, if only for a short distance. The group has to 'make' a monster, using everyone in the group, which will move a certain distance. The monster should have fewer legs than people: the fewer legs the harder it is (the group should say how many legs they are going for). Throw in the need for arms and strange voices to make it more fun.

Shepherd. A good exercise to get people planning and thinking things through. One person is nominated as a shepherd and the rest of the group are hence sheep! Give them a short planning time. All the sheep will then be blindfolded and the object of the activity is for the shepherd to herd the sheep into a pen. A rope on the floor with three sides closed and only one opening outline the pen. The shepherd can only use a whistle to direct the sheep, and they must stay by the 'pen'. Once planning time has been given the sheep are blindfolded and led away in different directions and spun to disorientate them.

Life raft. Quite a difficult exercise that requires planning and co-operation. The aim of the exercise is for the group to climb aboard the life raft, which can be anything from a circle on the floor to a slightly raised platform; obviously the smaller the circle, the harder the exercise. The team may not approach the raft during the planning stage but may practice away from the raft. Allow ten minutes or so for planning. Safety needs to be a priority: there should be no sitting on shoulders. The attempt will be judged a success when there are no parts of the group in contact with the floor outside the life raft for a period of five seconds (or more!). To demonstrate good planning the attempt must be made in silence.

Human knot. A simple exercise, often used as an icebreaker. The group stands in a circle, each person reaches into the middle and holds the left hand of another person and then the right hand of a third person. The group then has to 'untangle' the resulting knot without anybody letting go.

Chapter 7

Problem Solving and Decision Making

Problem solving can be one of the greatest challenges faced by a leader working with young people. Problem solving and making decisions can be a very new experience for many young people who are used to adults effectively making their decisions for them. This is particularly so given the busy nature of most people's lives, so that rather than take the time to work through a situation with young people they find it quicker and easier just to make the decision themselves. As a leader working with young people it is making this time that is at the cornerstone of the work you do. When new opportunities and excitements are encountered young people can be very enthusiastic and may demonstrate this through a surge of energy and endeavour. However, when hurdles are faced and problems encountered this energy can be short lived. Conversely, young people can be intimidated or feel overwhelmed by new situations and it is only when an element of success has been experienced that they start to commit to any new project. In addition it is rare, indeed very rare, that you will find a group of young people who are in complete agreement about anything. This is compounded to an even greater extent when decisions have to be made about future plans or intentions where members of a group have predetermined ideas. The opposite of this, which can be just as difficult, is where the young people involved have no idea and are quite happy to let someone else make the decision. If as a leader you accept that your job is to eventually step back and allow the young people in your care to make their own decisions (see Chapter 2 Vision and Styles and Chapter 3 The focus of leadership) then facilitating the problem solving process might just be the most important thing that you do as a leader. As Saul Alinsky (cited in Wheal 1998: pvii) points out:

> We learn, when we respect the dignity of the people, that they cannot be denied the elementary right to participate fully in the solutions to their own problems...To give people help, while denying them a significant part of the action, contributes nothing to the development of the individual.

Young people need to have the space and time to tackle problems in their own way rather than in a manner that an adult may deem appropriate. However, if and when their approach goes awry they will then need unconditional support and encouragement to learn from their mistakes and try again.

Bearing these issues in mind, this chapter can be read and used in different ways. As a leader working with young people you will undoubtedly have to solve a number of problems or, more usually, try to work out why something is not working as it should. Alternatively you might have to lead a group of young people through a problem solving process or help to resolve issues and difficulties that the young people in your care are experiencing. In any situation it is useful to have an idea of some of the established procedures and techniques that can be useful tools for the process of problem solving.

The Problem Solving Process

Where a team is involved in problem solving it is important that the team has a variety of people who are analytical, logical, creative and innovative. This underlines the importance of diversity within a team as discussed in the Teamwork chapter (Chapter 6). If however, a team is not involved the individual ideally needs to be able to bring the same variety of thought processes to the problem solving routine.

There are a number of stages that usually have to be fulfilled in order to solve a problem successfully. These stages can be individually addressed in sequence or responsibilities can be devolved to individuals or collective groups within a team. This may be a formal or informal process, which will largely depend on the nature of the people involved, and the style of leadership being adopted. The stages are:

Problem — information collecting

As much information as possible about the problem is gathered. Nothing can effectively be resolved until it is known what the problem is and what are the conditions, time, equipment, etc. connected to that task. Surprisingly this is the stage that is usually done badly with people and groups rushing into a task without having all the information they need. This can be overcome by:

Analysis — confirming

Not only should it be confirmed that all the information needed is available but it is also needs to be confirmed that every relevant person is aware of that information. The problem needs to be completely clarified at this stage and any unclear detail resolved or strategies put in place to cope with the unknown elements.

Alternatives — suggesting and sharing

This is where strategies for solving the problem are discussed and a number of alternative solutions are suggested and developed. This can be done formally with alternatives tabled and discussed in sequence or a 'brainstorming' technique can be used. The technique employed at this stage will reflect the nature of the group involved. Obviously for an individual brainstorming as a group may not be possible but a range of solutions can still be drawn up, figuratively or literally, and considered.

Evaluation

In order for the process to be effective some mechanism needs to be employed whereby each alternative put forward in the prior stage is examined in turn and its pros and cons debated. This stage needs to be comprehensive and systematic otherwise a choice could be made for the wrong reasons, often through it being suggested by a more forceful personality.

Decision

An alternative is chosen on its merits. This is the stage where the effective strategy and decisions are made, so it is important that there is agreement as to the way forward (see below Making the decision).

Planning

The decision once made needs to be followed by detailed planning; issues highlighted in the evaluation stage will influence this. In some ways this element of the problem solving process manages to be both the most important and the most neglected of all the stages in the process. A plan not only needs to contain what needs to be done and by whom but, most importantly, it needs to highlight by when. Timetabling and deadlines are essential in anything but the most simple of tasks. This is just as important for individuals as for groups. Timetables should be written down, precise and quantifiable. There should also be contingencies for any unsure elements.

Action

In this stage work commences on the chosen solution. It is important to ensure that not only does each individual member of the group have a role but that each of those individuals and the sub-groups in which they are working are aware of their place and function within the overall scheme. These sub-groups, individuals and their associated functions will need to be co-ordinated in order to get them to link together. For an individual this stage is slightly different because it is looking at the tasks, or components of tasks, that need to be done and asking *how* they will be done rather than *who* will do them. Building on the planning and co-ordinating phases is a need to ensure that specific people at selected places and times carry out specific actions. Everyone involved with the task needs to have a picture of the overall orientation of the task; this ensures continued motivation and commitment (see Chapter 4 Communication).

Re-evaluation

As work progresses the solution is monitored to ensure that it is fulfilling the criteria and adaptations made where necessary. There will always be a need to have ongoing monitoring, evaluation, re-evaluation and constructive criticism to ensure that unforeseen problems are dealt with and new challenges are met. This should include an ongoing monitoring of deadlines and contingencies.

These stages can be summed up by the model in Figure 15.

Although the loop consists of a number of stages it is immediately apparent that information is the central factor in each stage. This emphasises the importance of the information collecting stage described above.

The final stage, which is not shown on the loop because it follows the problem solving process, is reviewing where the process is examined in hindsight either in the form of a final review of a completed task or as an ongoing review of the process in preparation for the next task.

Making the Decision

Before going into the detail of decision making it is worth revisiting the role of the leader in this process (Chapter 2 Leadership styles). The 'authority' to make decisions can reside wholly with the leader, autocratic leadership, it can be shared with the group, democratic leadership, or it can be handed over entirely to the group, abdicratic leadership. In a similar manner the

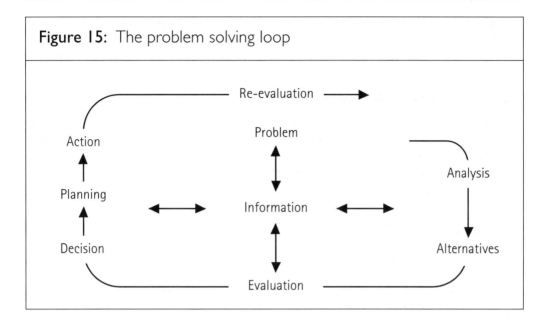

Figure 15: The problem solving loop

entire problem solving process can be managed by just the leader, the leader and the group or just the group. The emphasis on the process is the same as with leadership styles in any other situation. Where a quick decision is needed, rather than simply wanted, such as may be the case in an emergency or crisis, the leader should retain the authority to make the decision. Where the priority is group development and time and safety are not issues that need to be considered then the group can be left to make decisions. Sharing of decision making can be used where the group is in a formative stage (see Chapter 6 The stages of team development) or where all parties have a stake in the decision. It is important that it is made clear at the outset who will be involved in the decision making process and why.

There are essentially two ways to arrive at a solution and thereby a decision in any problem solving process; these are through being analytical or creative. This is where the team members with analytical/logical and creative/innovative skills mentioned at the start of the chapter come into play. In an ideal world the analytical people would go away, work through a logical, iterative process and come up with the same solution that the creative people came up with through the use of inspiration and innovation. In reality the type of problem that each skill is useful for is different to the extent that there would rarely be harmony and agreement between them. However, if a solution to a problem could be found to which both parties could agree then it can be reasonably certain that it has some merit.

There are a number of ways in which decisions can be reached and it is usually found that this is the hardest stage of the problem solving process. Given that there are a number of ways to reach a decision it can sometimes be that the hardest decision can be about the method to be used in making decisions! Completion of the task itself can sometimes be an anti-climax after the group has spent ages trying to decide on, often very trivial, procedures and designs.

It is possible for a leader to insist on a particular technique being used but it is usually best to allow a technique to be adopted by the young people involved and then examine its effectiveness in a subsequent review session. Having said this it is sometimes worth just reminding the group involved that the essence of teamwork is of a group of people working towards a common goal where each member of that team has a role to play. The following are the main types of decision making techniques.

Decision by lack of response

In this technique ideas are suggested and rejected in turn until an idea is proposed which is not objected to and is therefore adopted. The decision making process is essentially a negative one with ideas being rejected and the danger of associated hurt feelings on the part of the person submitting the idea. The solution arrived at is therefore often not the best one but simply the one to which the least people object to.

Decision by authority

This can either be through an elected leader making autonomous decisions or through group discussion with a chairperson having the final say or casting vote. Whilst highly efficient this technique can lead to group members feeling that they have been removed from ownership of the decision and therefore from a need to play a part in the task.

Decision by agreement

The perfect and most unlikely form of decision making is where everybody truly agrees with the course of action being proposed. Make the most of it when it happens but be suspicious, young people will often claim agreement merely to finish a fraught discussion and you can often find at a later date that some in the group actually disagreed with the decision and thus felt alienated from the proposed plan of action.

Decision by railroading

This is not the same as decision by authority; it is often carried through by not allowing any dissenting voices to be held and the use of such tactics as the quick vote or the suggestion that 'if no one objects lets get started' style of suggestion. This technique often comes about because of a bad, domineering, leadership style within the group.

Decision by majority vote

Usually done as either a first 'lets get the decision over with' ploy or as a last resort when a decision cannot be reached by other means. Its main hurdle is, of course, that the minority who voted against the motion will feel alienated from the subsequent action. This is, however, certainly the most common way of reaching a decision. It might be that if this technique is to be used that some ground rules such as a 'three-quarter majority is required' are set before the vote is taken. This can help to offset having a significant minority who do not agree with the decision.

Decision by consensus

This is probably the most time-consuming but most acceptable technique of reaching a decision. This technique is not the same as voting and reaching a majority because under a consensual agreement the case for different solutions are argued until everyone either agrees with a single solution or are at least happy to support it. The key to consensus is a group where everybody is able to express their own opinions and ideas without risk of confrontation.

Decision by compromise

This is a slightly watered down version of decision by consensus. In this case someone has agreed to a decision being accepted but without agreeing to the decision itself. This may often appear to be decision by consensus and can arise from an attempt to reach consensus but could in reality be where somebody has agreed merely in order to bring the discussion to an end. If a compromise decision is reached it must be open and voiced to avoid any resentments being secretly built up.

There is no right or wrong way to reach a decision, just as there is no right or wrong style of leadership. The technique used will vary and depend on the situation, the nature of the team and many other external and internal considerations.

As a leader of young people, however, you have to take a number of issues into consideration when the solution to a problem is put forward. Firstly, is it truly a solution to which all the young people can buy into or is it one that has been pushed forward by a domineering minority, and secondly is the solution actually feasible. If you are satisfied that these two are okay then you need to return to the wider responsibilities of a leader (see Chapter 14 The leader's responsibilities) to ensure that what is proposed will not cross any irredeemable or unacceptable boundaries.

Difficulties with Problem Solving

You may well find, as a leader facilitating a group of young people, that they often seem incapable of solving a problem or reaching a consensus on anything. This does not place you in a minority and you should not feel unduly alarmed by it; if anything it is the normal situation. It may be that even if all the correct procedures are followed there are still difficulties with a group of young people being unable to arrive at a solution for a problem or, alternatively, not being able to follow the solution through into action. These difficulties can be collected into five main areas or blocks; they are:

Technical

This refers to the problem not being approached through the correct use of the process outlined above. Examples of technical blocks include:

- Not being methodical.
- Not understanding the problem.
- Misinterpreting the problem.
- Using inappropriate techniques.
- Not having enough information.
- Not ensuring correct implementing of solution.

Perceptual

In this area there are difficulties with how the problem is perceived, either through preconceived ideas or not being able to recognise underlying issues. Examples include:

- Stereotyping.
- Mistaking cause and effect.
- Seeing what you expect, or want, to see.
- Not recognising that you are having difficulties.

Intellectual

The issue with these blocks is recognising that they exist and being able to take a step back from the problem to look at other ways of approaching it. It is often easier to recognise intellectual blocks from outside of the group. Examples of these might include:

- Lack of knowledge or skill.
- Inflexibility.
- Lack of creativity.
- Not being methodical.

Emotional

Often a major difficulty with young people, these blocks can be hidden and therefore more difficult to resolve than others. Careful facilitation and reviewing is often needed to resolve emotional blocks such as:

- Impatience.
- Lack of real challenge.
- Fear of taking risks.
- Fear of making mistakes.
- Fear of embarrassment, for oneself or others.

Expressive

Difficulties with communication and expression can be the death knell for problem solving and any form of group spirit. These blocks can often be linked to emotional blocks and should be approached in the same way, examples include:

- Inadequate information or reluctance to share information.
- Leadership within the group being too dominant or too passive.
- Language, usually technical, difficulties.

Frequently the solution to these blocks will require the leader to step in and instigate a re-evaluation of the group's progress in solving the problem (see Chapter 13 Evaluation). Whatever the block it can generally be overcome by facilitating one or more of the following:

- Observing and listening to fellow team members.
- Ongoing monitoring, reviews and comparisons.
- Rewards and recognition.
- Open and free communication.
- Sensible delegation.
- Lack of conflict and avoidance of confrontation.

- Showing commitment to innovation.
- Supportive team members.
- Giving ideas credit and avoiding criticism.

Conflict within groups will naturally arise and it is a large part of the work of a leader to be able to help young people resolve these. The key to resolving any conflict is positive and successful communication. There is also the need for the young people involved to be ready to compromise and accept others viewpoints as valid whilst at the same time being able to constructively examine their own contributions and behaviour. Wheal (1998: p18) suggests the following strategy:

- Awareness—being aware of the negative feelings of the situation.
- Self-preparation—separating the people from the problem; deciding what outcomes they require and understanding the reasons.
- Defusing negative emotions—each listening to the other person's point of view; this may not bring about settlement but will at least give an understanding of differences and a mutual respect for one another.
- Negotiation—enabling each party to achieve a mutually agreed outcome with respect for individual differences.

It is unlikely that a young person, particularly one who is fired up or agitated, will be able to go through such a process without calm mediation and facilitation from another person. It is important that this person is seen to have respect for the young person's viewpoint whilst at the same time remaining as neutral as possible in the resolution of the conflict. Very often it is simply the act of talking through a conflict or issue with another person that can lead to a young person, or group, being able to address a conflict in a calmer or more rational manner.

Problem Solving: *Activities*

There is a wide range of activities involving barrels, planks, bits of rope and imagined minefields and rivers which may on the face of it be about problem solving. In reality many of these activities, if not all of them are more to do with aspects of teamwork, communication and leadership than about solving the problem itself. A simple way of getting a group to arrive at a decision together is to give them a subject to discuss and agree on; one suggestion would be 'As a team, what do you need in life to be truly happy?' Obviously the answer to this is so individual that true agreement would be impossible so the range of decision making techniques discussed above could be employed. It has been known, particularly if majority voting is excluded, for this discussion to go on for hours and, if nothing else, for some fascinating subjects and insights to arise.

On a larger scale but perhaps somewhat more realistically there is little that will test a group's problem solving ability so much as completing a trip or expedition. This need not be anything adventurous; it could simply be a weekend trip to a neighbouring area. However, agreement will need to be reached regarding a destination, which will require information about the possible options; costs will need to be factored in, deadlines for making travel arrangements agreed and delegated; fund-raising might need to be planned and a whole host of other issues to be considered, agreed, planned and completed before even a simple trip can go ahead. Obviously organising anything more than the simplest of trips would in the first instance be a significant challenge for a first time project and would need careful leadership and guidance with the project broken down into easier and more manageable pieces.

Chapter 8

Learning

Only within yourself exists that other reality for which you long.
I can give you nothing that has not already its being within yourself...
All I can give you is the opportunity, the impulse, the key...
to make your own world visible.   Herman Hesse (1927) *Steppenwolf*

The leader of young people has some significant advantages over mainstream educators when working with young people. These usually, but not always, include:

- You are not tied to a rigid curriculum and your results, or more importantly the young person's results, are not tied into an assessment programme of exams and coursework.
- You are not tied to a classroom situation or timetable constraints.
- You have, or should have, a good relationship with the young people involved.
- They are not there because they have to be, and neither are you, there is generally enthusiasm on both sides.
- There is a more friendly and 'laid back' atmosphere.
- You probably have a good image with the young people. They do not see you so much as an authority figure but more as somebody who is there for them.
- The learning involved can be fun and novel.

All of these contribute in a significant manner to the efficacy of the learning experience. Significantly, when we look at how people learn, below, it is evident that the environment and atmosphere in which the leader of young people works is much more beneficial than the equivalent environment and atmosphere found within mainstream education. Furthermore, as Wurdinger (1997) points out, when a problem has direct relevance to the young people involved they become emotionally engaged in the learning process which, obviously, adds to the engagement with learning.

There is also the question of what type of learning the young people with you will be engaging in. Obviously, this is going to depend largely on the programme that you are working with. It may be issues connected with a particular group such as a young men or women's group; specific technical skills such as found on a Duke of Edinburgh's Award expedition group; general personal and social skills such as found in a youth group: the list goes on and on. The main feature, however, is that all of this learning can usually be seen as relevant by the young people involved; again very unlike the school environment.

Cooper (1998: p39) highlights the difference in styles between the leader as instructor and the leader as facilitator (Figure 16). This figure shows how the leader as instructor dominates the group so that despite getting good task related results, they do not encourage personal learning in the way that the leader as facilitator does. This goes to the heart of the learning process when working as a leader with young people (see also Chapter 2 Leadership styles).

It is because the leader working outside of the mainstream education system usually has the option of different styles and approaches that they can be so successful in getting young people to engage with the learning process. It is important, however, that the leader working with young people has an understanding of learning theories if they are to get the full benefit from their advantages.

Leader as Instructor	Leader as Facilitator
Figure 16: Approaches to learning (Cooper, 1998: p39)	
Instructor tells pupils	Leader shares with participants
Dominant	Participatory
Instructing: passing on knowledge and skills	Facilitating: encouraging participants to learn for themselves
Passive	Active
Task oriented	People oriented
Competitive	Co-operative
There is one approach to learning	There are a variety of approaches to learning
Terminology: instructor, tutor, students, pupils	Terminology: facilitator, guide, learners, participants
Emphasis on skills, competence	Emphasis on experience, reflection, learning
Emphasis on equipment as an aid	Emphasis on relationships as an aid

Why, and How, People Learn

There are a wide and enormously complex number of theories regarding how people learn. Cooper (1998: p40) presents evidence to suggest that young people learn best when:

- There is a problem to be solved.
- The learning is shared.
- They are involved in doing.
- The learning is related to their life.
- There is a challenge.
- There is time to reflect.
- They enjoy learning.

People learn in a number of ways but whichever way is used all learning will make use of a number of the six sense channels:

- sight
- hearing
- smell
- touch
- taste
- Muscle-memory (kinaesthetic)

The first key to really effective learning is to use as many of the sense channels as possible. There is a growing recognition that there are different learning styles which should be utilised to ensure effective learning. Some people, for example, like to try things for themselves, others like to listen, whilst others need to engage in debate. Whilst it is difficult to utilise specific learning styles to accommodate every young person in your group it is important to use a variety of 'teaching' styles, using as many of the sense channels as possible, so that everybody has the opportunity to get involved. So, for example, if running a coaching session, have some talk and listen, encourage questions, allow experimentation as well as guided practice and so on. Above all, the key to learning for young people is that it should be interesting, involving, relevant and motivating so that they want to learn.

This use of varied styles is particularly important when working with groups which include young people with learning support needs or difficulties. Almost unbelievably there are still cases of schools treating children with dyslexia, for example, as slow or even stupid. The leader of young people has the opportunity to help these young people by making them realise they are valued as equal to their peers. By not being tied to a rigid curriculum the leader can also encourage young people with learning support needs to make the most of the opportunities available to them and to look at alternative learning strategies:

> *When doing written work you have to use alternative words you can spell and not use the words you really want to use: it makes you feel different and left out. The teachers just said I was lazy and could try harder. I just wanted them to acknowledge that I was capable but simply couldn't spell.* (Janette, dyslexia sufferer)

Remember, however, that no one will learn anything if they are totally terrified. All outdoor instructors are familiar with the sensation of 'being gripped' basically this occurs when there is too much sensation and the body, and brain, freezes. Unlike being 'very scared' being 'gripped' is rarely, if ever, a useful learning experience and can be highly counter-productive. This sensation is not unique to outdoor activities, it might occur, for example, because a young person is new to a youth club, a team or activity. The important concern is that young people feel secure; obviously this can be a balancing act when they are also being challenged but the first step to feeling secure is to have faith in the leader.

Learning is most effective when an action or material is presented in manageable parts. This is the familiar breaking down of a technique into its parts that all instructors and coaches learn when training. There should be a period of consolidation, either mental or physical, between each part. Likewise the parts should follow a logical sequence and be placed within the context of the whole activity.

Logically following on from this; there needs to be a reason for learning. Telling a group that they need to learn how to make posters so that they can design the posters for a Friday disco is an obvious incentive for them to learn, whereas simply designing posters 'for the sake of it' is hardly inspiring. The leader should always, however, be aware of why people are on a course or at an activity in the first place as this may have a direct link to their desire and willingness to learn.

It is not always a natural process to associate facts and ideas. This explains the young person who simply cannot accept that a climbing rope is strong enough to hold them even though they have been told all the relevant figures. Using analogy, metaphor or simple examples are all effective ways of overcoming this, for example, rather than say 'this rope will hold so many kilograms' say 'this rope would easily lift this entire group' or 'because of the way this rope is made it is much stronger than this old style heavy rope'. The association of ideas makes the facts easier to accept.

If students are well motivated and interested in what they are doing then obviously the learning process is much easier. In any instance, however, the following techniques will always make learning more interesting:

Questions and answers are far more effective and interesting than one way 'lecturing'.

Discussion is often needed because few subjects will be cut and dried with no issues to be resolved. Discussion also helps young people to not only learn from the leader but also from each other.

Exercises are a good way of maintaining interest. Practice of each part of a new mental or physical skill is far more effective than waiting in silence and then practising the whole skill. Repetition of a physical exercise also overcomes the inherent short-term normal memory by making use of the much more effective muscle-memory.

Variety, because variety is the spice of life! However learning one new skill immediately after learning another one can be counter-productive as the earlier skill will be forgotten. There needs to be alternation between old and new skills.

Learning Cycles

It is important to consider, when facilitating learning with young people, the purpose of that learning. Gass (1985) discusses three ways in which learning can be transferred from one situation to another. These are:

Specific transfer

This is where a learner learns a particular skill which can be directly applied to a different situation. An example of this could be learning to tie knots in a rock climbing session and then being able to use them for sailing.

Non-specific transfer

In this instance it is not a skill that is transferred but a principle or process. Problem solving is a good example of this type of transfer where the process used to solve a maths problem might also be used to devise a football league.

Metaphoric transfer

This is where the transfer is of an attribute or personal characteristic between entirely different situations. In this, for example, the determination to finish a Duke of Edinburgh's Award might be transferred to finding a job. It is this type of transfer, and learning, that is commonly referred to on youth development programmes. By bearing in mind the different types of transfer a leader can help young people make connections with their learning which will engage them and help to build motivation.

The modern originator of experiential learning, John Dewey (1938) put forward the basic principles of effective learning as:

- Start with the learner. Consider their knowledge, skills, interests and needs.
- Learning is social and should involve group interaction.
- The learning process is an interaction with their environment.
- Learning needs to engage in problem solving.
- Experience should be reviewed and new learning transferred to future situations.

It can be seen from this that experiential education, essentially learning utilising experience and experimentation, is despite its apparently unstructured style, organised and structured with planned reviewing, reflection and transfer of learning. The most common learning model used to demonstrate this in experiential education is that of learning cycles. The popularity of these are two-fold, firstly they are simple, elegant yet effective and, secondly, they show clearly the progression of learning which typifies this style of work. There are many forms of learning cycles but essentially, in recent terms, the most well-known is based on the work of Kurt Lewin, cited by Kolb (1984), shown in Figure 17.

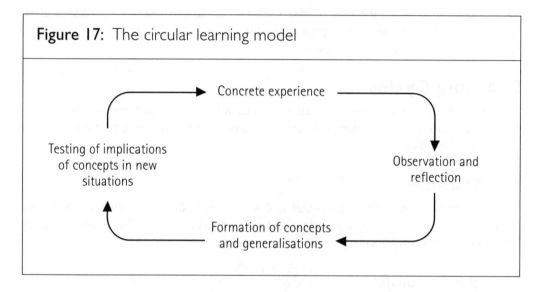

Figure 17: The circular learning model

The four stages in the cycle can be simply described as:

Something happens—What happened?—What did it mean?—What now?

For sheer simplicity, elegance and effectiveness there is little that can beat this model. Not only is the learning cycle model seen as the basis for experiential learning it can also be used as the structure for reviewing activities and tasks (see Chapter 9 Reviewing and Feedback). It is also very effective when used for briefing students at the start of an exercise or activity. Kolb's circular pattern has formed the basis for many other circular patterns, for example Outward Bound staff have traditionally used a circle of 'Plan, Do, Review' to describe the learning process on their courses. This simple and effective model can be expanded into a spiral to give the model shown in Figure 18.

The advantages of this experiential style of learning closely reflects the list given at the start of this chapter and from the viewpoint of the learner benefits from (Cooper, 1998: p42):

- Motivating the learner. People enjoy active learning.
- Using co-operative learning, there is a sharing of knowledge and experience.
- Utilising different learning styles.
- Learning is transferred from one situation to another.
- Being democratic by empowering people to take responsibility for their own learning.

The spiral model is now rapidly replacing the traditional circular learning model which could be taken to imply that skills are not transferable to situations outside of the circle. A much more elaborate spiral model, is shown in Figure 19. This model shows that behaviour is followed by

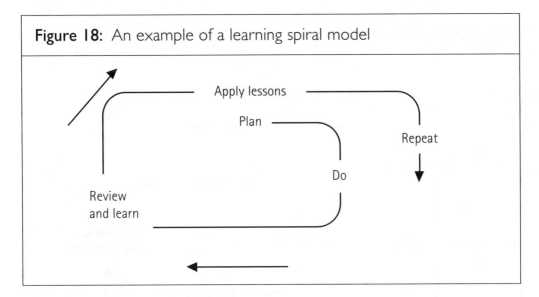

Figure 18: An example of a learning spiral model

a period of reflection at which point a decision is made. If the behaviour is accepted than a traditional learning cycle of 'what happened' and through to 'what next' and implementing those lessons is followed. If the behaviour is rejected then the inner circle continues until an increase in experience allows that behaviour to become acceptable, or new behaviour learnt, and the larger spiral to be entered.

How People Perceive Themselves

One of the prime objectives of working with young people is to get them to see themselves for what and who they really are. It is only when this self-honesty is achieved that truly effective personal development can take place.

The Johari Window

One very powerful model to help with demonstrating this self-perception is the 'Johari Window'. The word 'Johari' is a derivative of the names of Joseph Luft and Harry Ingham who developed the model as a technique for reducing interpersonal conflict in the 1960s (Luft, 1961). In its purest form the model is shown, in Figure 20 as a four windowed box.

The key element of the window is that it relates to self and how the individual, 'you' in this example, perceives others' perception of themselves. The common technique of using the window to show the perceptions of others is not strictly correct but is a development of the original idea and is dealt with later. In the standard model the four elements are:

Open self—in which you are aware of how you affect others and you are also aware of other's impact on you. In addition others are aware of your knowledge. In this scenario there is nothing hidden and, therefore, little risk of interpersonal conflict.

Hidden self—where you are aware of your feelings and intentions and how you impact on others. However, you are not aware of the others' reaction to you. In this scenario you do not reveal your true feelings in order to avoid conflict. This may lead to mistrust on the part of others.

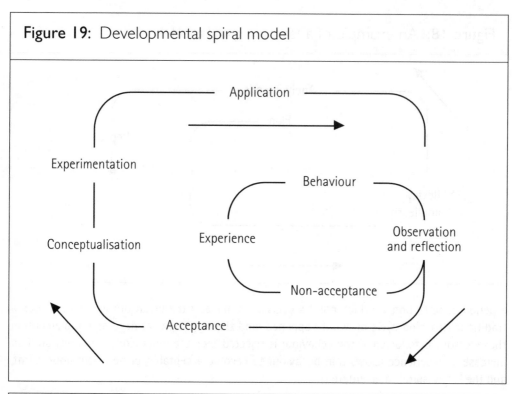

Figure 19: Developmental spiral model

Application

Experimentation

Behaviour

Conceptualisation   Experience   Observation and reflection

Non-acceptance

Acceptance

Figure 20: Johari's Window

	You do know about the other	You do not know about the other
You do know about yourself	**Open self**	**Hidden self**
You do not know about yourself	**Blind self**	**Undiscovered self**

Blind self—in this situation you are aware of others but you are unaware of how you may be affecting them. It may be that you are unintentionally irritating them. If you are open to feedback this situation can be resolved otherwise it may lead to conflict.

Undiscovered self—here you are not only unaware of how you affect others, the impact you have on them, but you are also unaware of the others' motives and intentions. This is a volatile situation with plenty of scope for interpersonal misunderstanding and conflict.

It can be seen that one of the difficulties with the Johari's Window model is that it requires a degree of convoluted thought in order to really get to grips with its true implications. Probably

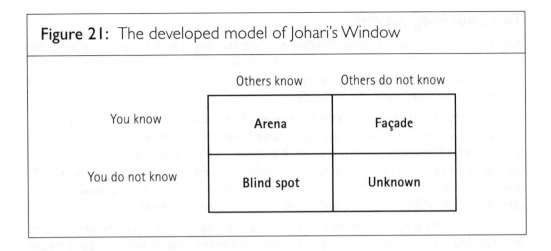

Figure 21: The developed model of Johari's Window

because of this it is often adapted to the model shown in Figure 21. This model is not talking about a person's own perception of self and others but rather how things may be viewed from both the perspective of self and of others.

In the developed model the four elements are:

Arena—things about your personality that you know and others know, you will recognise a description of yourself given by the other.

Façade—things you know and others don't know, you will be keeping aspects of your personality hidden to avoid conflict.

Blind spot—things others know about you that you don't know, these may be positive or negative and feedback will be required to highlight them to avoid conflict.

Unknown—things about you that you don't know and others don't know, joint awareness needs to be nurtured through activity, feedback and reviewing.

The features of the developed model are rather simpler to grasp, for example, an individual may be unaware of an irritating habit, or 'blind spot', which is obvious to others and needs to be pointed out to him. The Johari's Window, in both its forms, makes the elegant learning point that: everyday life can be said to exist in the 'facade' and 'blind spot' areas with most people being private about their innermost thoughts and feelings, about themselves and others in much the same way as normal everyday conversation is carried on at the 'cocktail' level.

The leader working with young people should be encouraging and facilitating them to explore their 'unknown/undiscovered self', move through the 'blind self/spot', be open about the 'hidden self/facade' and operate in the 'open self/arena' window. It is by doing this that the self-development element with young people starts to work. Many things have to come together for people to move into the 'open self/arena' window but the most important of them is for a person to be honest with themselves. A group, or team, which has successfully moved a number of issues out of the less open windows will be operating at a higher level of communication, because there are fewer secrets and hidden agendas, as well as a higher level of functioning as a group. The energy of the group (see Chapter 6 Characteristics of effective teams) can be directed to the task in hand rather than preserving hidden areas and identities.

The coaching model

Another development of the Johari Window can be combining it with a learning cycle to give the model in Figure 22. In simple terms this model, which is often used in sports coaching, suggests that we have to know that we can't do something, 'conscious incompetence', before we can learn the skills needed to do it well.

This cycle can be related to the gathering of experience and confidence on an activity course. To give an example, someone may attend a course having no idea about tennis (unconscious incompetence) they will try it, find it difficult and the leader or instructor will have to show them what they are doing wrong (conscious incompetence). By learning these lessons and with practice they will develop the skills of a tennis player (conscious competence) and with further experience those skills will become instinctive (unconscious competence).

Not only can this model be applied to activity or sports skills such as tennis, the same lessons can be applied to learning about personal habits, traits and abilities and the self-perception needed to do that. It emphasises the point that learning can often be a difficult experience because the first stage has to be admitting that either something is unknown or that something needs changing.

It is frequently the role of the leader working with young people to address the area of unconscious incompetence, or blind spot, with the people they work with. This will require the skilled use of activity, feedback and review (Chapter 9) as well as learning styles and self-perception awareness. By using all the advantages at their disposal, outlined at the start of this chapter, the leader of young people has a possibly unique opportunity to assist young people to move their learning about themselves, and others, forwards in a positive and constructive manner.

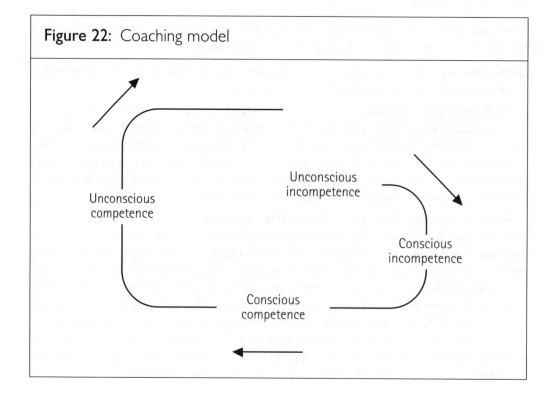

Figure 22: Coaching model

Chapter 9

Reviewing and Feedback

This chapter builds on the previous chapter on learning and many of the models used in that chapter are equally relevant here; Johari's Window being a good example of a learning model which is equally relevant to reviewing and feedback. Reviewing and feedback, as with reviewing and evaluation (Chapter 13) are often confused. The difference is however simple, reviewing is about the young person discovering things about themselves through talking, usually, following an experience whilst feedback is the young person being told about themselves. It is common for feedback sessions to become reviewing sessions but this chapter treats the two as being completely distinct from each other.

Reviewing

Reviewing can be seen in two ways both of which have their devoted supporters. Firstly it can be argued that an experience is totally self-contained and needs no elaboration. This was certainly the argument of the early educationalists who believed that 'the experience was everything' and talking about it was a waste of time. The second argument is that an experience is nothing unless it is discussed, analysed and related back to everyday life. It is this process, it is argued, which gives the experience its meaning. Dewey (1916: p78) the 'father' of experiential education wrote that:

> One may learn by doing something which he does not understand; even in the most intelligent action, we do much which we do not mean, because the largest portion of the connections of the act we consciously intend are not perceived or anticipated. But we learn only because after the act is performed we note results which we had not noted before.

The reality is, of course, that the answer lies between the two extremes, although probably more to the 'talking' side. Too much talking can detract from the experience whilst no talking can render it meaningless. What is certainly true, however, is that reviewing done badly can at best be a waste of time and at worst can be extremely harmful.

Reviewing serves many purposes. It can be quite deep and intense and used to explore emotions or strong feelings. For the purpose of much of the work with young people, however, reviews are used to firstly make sense of, and develop, what has just happened in an activity and secondly to carry the lessons learnt forward into the next activity, everyday life, the workplace or life development. In a rather simplistic sense reviews exist to make people think about what has happened. This reflects the original philosophy of experiential education. For Dewey (1916; 1938) learning was only effective if a connection was made between what happened and what were the learning consequences and, more importantly, between one experience and the next (this is reflected in the learning spiral, Chapter 8). Learning without these connections Dewey saw as compartmentalised and only of limited value.

Reviewing myths

There are many myths surrounding reviewing, these are some of the more common:

The review is the serious bit of the course

The idea that reviewing needs to consist of a group of people sitting in a circle earnestly discussing the meaning of life is not only wrong it is responsible for more bad reviews than almost anything else. Reviews can be fun!

The review takes place at the end of an activity

There is no need for a review to take place at the end of a session or activity: it can take place after, during or even before (this is called front-loading) a session.

The review needs to be a formal session

Nothing could be further from the truth; there is no need for reviews to be formal. Holding a review over dinner or whilst sitting around a campfire can be far more productive than sitting around a table. Likewise a purely informal sharing of the day's highlights with lots of loud voices and laughter can not only be a great review it can also be a great way to end a day.

The review involves the whole group

Often it may be simply inappropriate to involve the whole group. Asking a small sub-group why they are watching an activity rather than taking part can lead to a valuable on the spot review that may salvage an entire course.

The review is all about talking

Some of the best reviews involve little or even no talking. Don't be afraid to use drawing, acting or mime to explore themes, often people are more comfortable with using mediums other than talking.

Each activity needs reviewing

There will be times when the group is so active and on such a high that to force them to stop and discuss what is happening could stop the flow. Save the ideas, note them down perhaps, and review later if this is happening.

A review should have a set finishing time

There are mixed views on this. Certainly some people, if allowed, will happily talk all night and perhaps they do need some structure or a time-limit setting. However if genuinely useful or important ideas are being raised then it may be a mistake to finish because the clock says so. Another danger with setting a time is that some people may not get a chance to speak or even worse they may emotionally open themselves up and then be left hanging with no conclusion to the discussion.

Reviewing is difficult

Whilst reviewing should not be thought of as easy it is nothing to be scared of. Following a few simple guidelines, such as the four stage reviewing technique described below, can make all the difference. Reviewing is, however, a skill and needs to be learnt in exactly the same way as coaching a football technique or paddling a kayak.

Reviews are emotional

People should not be forced to reveal their deepest emotions just because a misguided reviewer believes that the review is a failure unless everyone is in tears. Some reviews will be emotional but there is no need for every review to be so, indeed it will often be completely inappropriate.

A few basic rules for effective reviewing

Every activity needs some rules and reviewing is no different. Many of the rules are in reality guidelines but they should be adhered to unless there is a good reason why not. Many of these rules can be put forward to the group as 'ground rules' for a review session. It is, however, better if a group of young people set their own ground rules at the start of a review or session; you need to ensure, by 'sleight of hand' that the following are included:

Reviews are confidential

In some review situations people will reveal their feelings, emotions and history more than is usual. Anything that is revealed in this way should be regarded as confidential just as if it was in a counselling session or a medical interview (but see Chapter 12 Looking After Yourself and Others).

Reviewing demands respect

There can be few things worse in life than being laughed at or put down when putting forward a contribution to a discussion. Everyone in the review group has an absolute right to be listened to with respect.

A review is not for someone to show off their knowledge

There is a danger, particularly, for younger leaders, to use review sessions to show how clever they are. When someone starts spouting off theories and ideas without input from the rest of the group it becomes a lecture not a review.

Everyone has an opinion

A review must not be monopolised by one or two people, there should be an opportunity for anyone, who wants to, to speak. Even more importantly other group members need to listen to their opinions.

No one can be forced to give an opinion

If someone does not want to speak they should not be forced to. Hopefully the group will be supportive enough that no one feels too intimidated to speak.

Reviews should be positive

Although not everything that happens during an activity or a course will be positive it is important that the review does more than just highlight negative features. No person, or group, should ever be knocked down if they are not then picked back up. If it is at all possible every review should end on a positive note even if it is only 'well; we are all agreed that was rubbish but at least we know why it was so bad. So now we can improve on it by using those lessons we've just learnt'.

The reviewer needs to be responsive

In the ideal world the reviewer will not force opinions or lead groups into discussions. They will rather respond to the group's needs and allow them to draw out lessons and issues. Although the reviewer may have to keep a session 'on track' they should be stimulating discussion rather than leading it.

The four stage reviewing system

A useful framework to base a review on is that suggested by Roger Greenaway (1993). Not everyone will like the idea of such a formal framework but it is important in even the most informal and 'on the hoof' review to have a clear idea of what you are doing. The four stage sequence is one technique for doing that. It is not suggested here that the framework is adhered to rigidly with allocated time slots for each stage, but rather it is used as a guideline. Based on the learning cycle, it consists of experience, express, examine and explore stages:

The experience stage concentrates on what happened? It can be likened to gathering evidence to serve as a reminder. Often a good way of doing this is for people to talk through what they felt happened; this often leads to other group members being surprised at how others' perceived the same incidents.

The express stage asks how did it feel? This stage is a vital one but can often be glossed over because of time constraints or because group members are finding it difficult to express their emotions.

The examine stage is the analytical stage that asks what do you think? It seeks to rationalise what happened. Inexperienced reviewers sometimes tend to jump straight to this stage in an attempt to keep the 'buzz' of the activity going—this is usually a mistake.

The explore stage is more practical and asks what next? This stage applies the lessons learnt from the experience and moves them forward or translates them into some meaning in everyday life.

Some hints for reviewing

Whilst this chapter is not an all-inclusive guide to reviewing there are some techniques that are worth being aware of.

Front-loading

Some people may not regard this as a review technique because it comes before an activity but it is all part of the ongoing review process. In essence it consists of asking questions such as 'what are we going to do?', 'how are we going to do it?', 'what do we need to bear in mind?', 'what fears do people have about doing this?' and so on. A front-loading session can follow a very similar format to an end of session review but with the added bonus that people will be thinking about the issues whilst doing the activity thereby having more to contribute to a later review session. Questions and issues (Priest and Gass, 1994) that might be raised by front-loading include:

- Revisit—what lessons where learnt from the last activity.
- Objectives—what is the aim of the next activity and what can be learnt from it.
- Motivation—why is the activity important and how does it relate to everyday life.
- Function—what behaviour and actions will help to bring about success and how best to use them.
- Dysfunction—what behaviour and actions will hinder success and what to do about them.

Metaphor

Metaphors have many uses but their main purpose is to provide a platform for relating the experience in question back to the everyday life of the students. Metaphors can be immediately obvious such as 'we are going to build a raft which is similar to putting together a project back in the workplace' or more subtle such as the old favourite 'climbing a mountain is like life itself, sometimes you have to get through the clouds to see where you are going'. Metaphors used in this way can be extremely powerful, they can also be extremely silly if used constantly and inappropriately.

Metaphors can also be used for individual descriptions, for example 'if you were a car or a tree or a plant or a house, what would you be and why?' might produce the answer 'I would be a Volvo because I like to think of myself as steady and dependable'. The same technique can also be used to get group members to describe each other; this is often a very effective way of overcoming people's embarrassment at talking about each other.

Physical reviewing

This means that people actually move to express their feelings. Physical reviewing can be a fun way of getting people involved who might otherwise sit there in silence. It can be as simple as standing up to express happiness and sitting down to express sadness. It can also be more complex with people moving around to stand in different places to show their feelings. For example, an outline of a swimming pool can be laid out with people standing in the 'deep end' to show they are fully involved or standing in the 'shallow end' to signify that they are unsure of committing themselves. Obviously such an activity requires a large amount of individual interpretation, standing at the 'deep end', for example, may signify to some people that they are out of their depth!

The use of drama

Drama can be a lot of fun, particularly for children who can act out a situation rather than sitting around and describing it. The drama need not be a literal report of an event, a group might be asked to provide a dramatic interpretation of lessons learnt during an activity. In this way the review itself becomes another activity.

Drawing

The type of drawing need not be a picture, it might be in the form of a map showing the 'journey' undertaken during an activity or it could consist of symbolic pictures each with a theme. The effectiveness of this type of reviewing is shown by its popular use as a form of counselling and therapy. It is important that the person who drew the picture is allowed to interpret it rather than other people drawing their interpretations and possibly reading things into the drawing that were never intended.

Chuff charts

Often known as 'highs and lows' this simply entails going through an activity and scoring moments during it on certain criteria such as how scary or how much fun. This technique can be very effective if group members do their own chuff charts and then compare them followed by a discussion of the differences.

Feedback

Giving feedback to young people can be one of the hardest parts of a leader's job. Surprisingly even giving positive feedback can be difficult because, as with negative feedback, it involves overcoming our natural barriers when it comes to telling other people what we think, or know, about them.

There are a number of scenarios in which feedback may need to be given. These could include:

- A formal interview at the end of a programme.
- Passing on problems with someone that other people have highlighted.
- Encouraging young people to give feedback to each other to move a group or project forward.
- Telling someone that their behaviour or attitude is inappropriate.
- Helping someone to improve either in a physical, life or social skill.
- Resolving issues within a group.

Whatever the situation feedback has essentially four main functions:

- To give information, usually about a performance or outcome.
- To provide positive or negative reinforcement.
- To justify some form of punishment or sanction.
- To provide motivation.

Given that feedback can be a difficult skill to acquire there are a few pointers that can make it both easier and more effective.

Be clear about what you are intending to say

Particularly if you are nervous it is important to have a clear idea of what you are going to say, practice or write it down if necessary. It can also be very useful to check with a colleague if what you are going to say is appropriate and in context. It would not be unusual for the person giving feedback to be emotionally involved with what is happening and another person can give a more objective view.

Start with the positive aspects of what you need to say

There is a general habit of stating the negative whilst forgetting the positive. Everyone needs encouragement and support, even if they are being disciplined in some way. If positive aspects are emphasised first the person receiving the feedback is more likely to listen to, and act upon, any more negative element of the message.

Be specific

Particularly with young people it is very important to be specific. It is no use at all simply saying 'your behaviour is unacceptable', the young person involved will reject this message as irrelevant and will probably challenge it; possibly leading to a defensive situation (see Chapter 4 Non-verbal communication). Being specific with feedback also increases the opportunity for learning and achieving a positive outcome to the situation. In a similar vein feedback given collectively to a group of people will very rarely be effective unless specific incidents and people are mentioned, the normal, very human, response to general feedback is to assume that it is being delivered at someone else. Incidentally, this applies to positive feedback, or praise, as well as negative feedback.

Select priorities

Giving a large amount of feedback in one go will dilute the message to such an extent that none of it will be effectively considered. It is far better to select the major, priority, issues and leave the smaller issues to one side.

Concentrate on the behaviour rather than the person

It is important not to concentrate on what it is about a person that is the difficulty but what that person does. For example, it would not be beneficial to say 'you're a really bossy person' it would be far better to say 'you are inclined to take charge a lot without giving other people a chance.' This moves the criticism away from the personal.

Concentrate on what can be changed

The purpose of feedback is to bring about a change, so concentrating on aspects or issues that cannot be changed is both futile and counter-productive. In the example above being a bossy person is a personal trait that the person involved would dismiss as being unchangeable but letting other people have a go at leading is something that can be managed.

In addition to these features of useful feedback it is also important that the appropriateness of the feedback is considered.

Is it the right time?

This can mean; is it the right time for both the leader and/or the young person? The leader might be too wound up or even angry whilst the young person might be too upset or emotionally involved. It is, however, important that feedback is given as close to the event in question as possible if the message is to be effective.

Is it the right place?

The setting can play a considerable part in the content of a message. A very formal feedback situation can be emphasised by holding it in an office setting whilst a more informal message can be emphasised by sitting side by side in the canteen. There is also the question of privacy and should the setting be away from others or, if others are involved, should it be more public. In general any negative or serious feedback should be considered confidential and delivered in private. This can be turned into a positive feature by saying that the feedback is just between the two people involved and no one else need know about it (assuming that this is appropriate and there are no formal procedures or paperwork to be completed).

Is it the right person?

It may be that the leader involved is not the best or most appropriate person to give feedback. A situation might be serious enough to warrant this being emphasised by a manager of some sort delivering the message or it might be that the leader involved is too close to the situation or emotionally involved.

How to do it?

Avoid being evasive, if feedback has to be delivered, for whatever reason, follow the guidelines above, avoid being obviously nervous and confront the situation.

Feedback can be avoided for a number of reasons but there are usually good reasons why it needs to be undertaken. Positive feedback can be avoided or neglected because of embarrassment or simply forgotten in the excitement of the moment. It can also be that we don't actually like the person involved and we don't want to give them any reason to become conceited; whilst this is perfectly human, it is, of course, unprofessional. With negative feedback it can be because we don't want to upset someone or we feel uncomfortable about having to deal with what might be a difficult situation involving distress or even anger. It is important, however, to consider the implications of not giving feedback. A situation can continue to build up until a major confrontation is unavoidable or it may be that a person's behaviour never changes simply because they are unaware of what they are doing (see Johari's Window and the coaching model in Chapter 8). It can also lead to a continuing decline in a relationship between the leader and a young person or between members of a group when addressing the issue might resolve it and lead to a positive relationship in the future. For all these reasons feedback needs to be delivered, ideally by someone who has a positive relationship with the young person involved and who is both skilled in giving feedback and empathetic with the feelings of the young person.

Chapter 10

Different Groups, Different Needs

Introduction

It is all too easy to split young people into different groups and then treat those groups as if they were entirely different with entirely different needs. It is important to bear in mind that groups are made up of individuals and that individuals within groups may have little in common with each other and may indeed resent being labelled as part of a group. To discuss young women, for example, as though there were no differences between them is, of course, extremely difficult. To take a clichéd example; a young Asian woman from a deprived inner-city background may well have more in common with a young male from the same background than with a young Anglo-Saxon woman from an affluent family in the countryside. However, having said this there are common traits within groups that may require consideration from a leader. This chapter looks at leadership considerations with the groups most usually considered as having identifiable needs. It starts with the oldest distinction of all, the difference between men and women.

It will hardly come as a shock to anyone that young men and women are different but as leaders it is important that this difference is handled sensitively. A common mistake in working with young people is to recognise the differences that exist and then to ignore them until an incident slaps you in the face. Young people relate to the world around them in a number of stereotypical ways that need to be taken into account not least in the way they perceive themselves:

> ...it is important to understand the impact of socially constructed meaning on later social interaction...Our notion of gender is one of the key components of our self-concept.
>
> (Rea and Slavkin, 2000: p89)

It is interesting to note that even young women who are assertive amongst their peer group can take a back role when in a mixed group where the males in the group are perceived as 'dominant':

> It was important for girls to work together in a group because there are no boys to butt in and take over. You can also bond better together than boys can when they are together, alone.
>
> (Laura, 11 and Tasha, 12)

Young men on the other hand who may be quiet amongst their peers can become loud and 'boorish' or 'show-offs' when working with young women: much to the annoyance of others:

> We wouldn't be able to do most activities if boys were around, because if we were doing the ropes the boys would be on it most of the time.
>
> (Hannah, 9)

Obviously these are sweeping statements to make but it is worthwhile to note how often gender stereotypes are reinforced in a group situation. Camping is a good example of how people can tend to gravitate to their stereotypical roles with men putting up the tents whilst the women get on with the cooking. As Warren (1996: p12) says of this situation:

> ...the most expedient way to set up camp is for people to do the tasks that are comfortable and familiar to them. In spite of our noble intentions of egalitarianism, when efficiency is important in a trying situation women often do end up cooking.

Obviously while it is always worthwhile challenging stereotypes amongst young people the ideal time to break established stereotypical behaviour is before a pattern is well-established; or even formed in the first place.

Leadership with young women

Leadership with young women can represent a number of challenges; these may well be different and dependant on a number of factors. Not surprisingly the gender of the leader can make a difference although not always in obvious ways. Young women will probably be very unlikely to discuss anything to do with their menstrual cycle with a male leader for example and often young women (and young men as well) will need their own space where they can talk openly:

> *I couldn't talk about stuff if boys were there.* (Lacey, 11)

Male leaders may find that they are barred from conversations or excluded in ways that might seem hurtful. The reality is usually that they have simply come too close to a gender barrier and the exclusion is nothing personal, although knowing this may not help the uncertainty that can arise in a male leader's mind. One thing that does remain certain, however, is that young women remain on the whole very aware of their femininity and their difference from young men. To what extent this is playing a socially acceptable role is difficult to say. Rea and Slavkin (2000) in their work found that young women would often say things to maintain a socially acceptable gender identity but actually act in a contradictory manner. This would seem to indicate, in this instance at least, that it was the imperative to appear feminine which was socially ingrained rather than the need to actually act in a feminine manner. The lesson in this for leaders is that the block on some activities for young women (and probably men) may be in the social perception of that activity and its acceptability as a suitable activity for young women rather than in the activity itself.

The contribution by Di Collins later in this chapter looks at this difference in one of the most established of male territories, the outdoors.

Working with people with disabilities or special needs

A mystique has unfortunately grown up around working with people with disabilities. Many of us are torn between being frightened of working with disabled people and being full of admiration for those that do. In essence this goes to the heart of working with disabled people; 'they' are people like us who simply have some special needs to be accommodated. Young people with disabilities nearly always have the same physical, social and emotional needs as any other young person; and all the same problems and confusions. It is important when working with young people with special needs that they are given the same rights and respect as any other young people. Such practical things as talking directly to them instead of to carers, allowing them the same personal space and dignity as any other person and not making assumptions about them are all important. They should also be given the same expectations, opportunities and boundaries as their 'able-bodied' peers and allowed to make their own mistakes in the same way.

Unfortunately a lot of the conflict in working with young people with disabilities has been bought about by the experts themselves who have developed a language and culture that can be seen to intimidate those not in the know. Wheal (1998) gives a very good example of a politically correct organisation insisting on the term 'with disabilities' whilst a disabled person had no problem with being called disabled and indeed saw it as the most apt description for herself. Obviously words such as spastic, invalid, mental and Mongol have now all rightly been consigned to history and it is important that derogatory terms such as these are avoided. More importantly however it is essential that, whilst not denying the special needs of people with disabilities, we recognise them as individuals without being frightened of occasionally doing or saying something wrong:

> *I just want people to talk to me as a normal person, they don't have to be scared of me just*
> *because I look a bit different; I'm still human.* (Paul, a wheelchair user)

As a footnote to working with young people with disabilities or special needs we often talk about working with these groups or with 'able-bodied' groups but rarely do we talk about working with mixed groups. This is actually far more likely in a situation such as running something like a youth group. It is worth considering that many young people will be embarrassed not so much by disabled people as by their own reactions to them. They will be reluctant to make the first step because they feel out of their depth or unsure about how to act. You, as a leader, need to show them that they can act towards a disabled person in the same way as they would act towards any one else: perhaps just with a little bit more consideration.

The contribution by Phil Woodyer later in this chapter highlights some of the practical implications of working with groups with special needs or disabilities. He, quite rightly, makes the point that there are many varieties and levels of special needs, which need an equally varied amount and type of support.

Leadership with people from ethnic communities

Of all the groups identified as having their own needs people from ethnic communities are probably one of the most diverse and yet, ironically, the most likely to be 'lumped together'. Young people from ethnic 'minority' groups could be from a number of diverse cultures, religions and backgrounds, they could be from first, second or third (or more) generations new to this country, English may or may not be their first language and, depending on where they live, they may be in the minority or the majority in their local community. And all this is on top of differences such as gender, class, education and so on. However it is almost certainly true that (Williams, cited in Webb, 2001: p9):

> *The simple matter of the colour of one's skin so profoundly affects the way one is treated,*
> *so radically shapes what one is to think and feel about this society, that the decision to*
> *generalise from such a division is valid.*

There is a concern that through the simple process of 'targeting' a group such as young people from ethnic communities they are automatically marginalised with the differences between 'them' and 'us' emphasised, rather than the diversity that exists in society as a whole. It is also true, however, that people, and especially young people from ethnic communities are still likely to face discrimination in their dealing with authority, public and professional life. They are also far more likely to be amongst the more deprived or underachieving members of our society. The leader working with young people from ethnic communities therefore has a difficult balancing act to fulfil. They will need to recognise and celebrate diversity within various parts of society whilst at the same time recognising that some of those same groups will be marginalised by virtue of that very diversity.

This balancing act can take the form of appreciating the ways you work with people from different ethnic and cultural backgrounds. Simple practical things such as referring to 'first' names rather than 'Christian' names or not making assumptions about religion or 'countries of origin' are important. Conversely you may need, as a leader, to look more at ways in which your organisation or local community works or how certain groups work together.

The contribution later in this chapter by Judy Ling Wong addresses some of these wider issues.

Working with Young Women in the Outdoors: *Di Collins*

Maria waits at the edge of the group: accepted by the group but never a real member of the group. She watches as the other young women tackle the high ropes course, shouting encouragement to each other. She feigns a headache and sits down. When they take off their equipment and move on to their next activity, she hangs behind. With the leader's encouragement she walks a short way along the log. A smile crosses her face.

There are many Marias in the world (and many Marks). Why would she not tackle the high ropes course when the rest of the group were present to encourage her? Would Maria have attended an outdoor residential experience, had it been as a member of a mixed group? What did she gain from this experience?

When young people engage in outdoor education experiences, their involvement may be influenced by at least three factors:

- How they feel about themselves.
- How they feel about themselves with the group and how they think the group feels about them.
- How they feel about the activity, their perceptions of what that activity involves and their ability to do it.

Many young people experience low self-esteem, a poor self-image and a lack of confidence. The Erikson model of psychosocial development suggests that during adolescence, young people may have another chance, another opportunity to redefine themselves as they struggle with being industrious versus feeling inferior, and identity development versus role confusion (Sugarman, 1986). Outdoor education may have a critical role to play in this phase of life development. It can give young people opportunities to explore the self and the self and the group, in an environment that has different challenges from those they might face at home. Hopkins and Putnam (1993) argue that outdoor education provides an effective learning environment for personal and social development.

However, perceptions of the outdoors and outdoor activities may block participation. Some young women, particularly urban young women, may have no real concept of the outdoors. For them it may be the formal plantings or a few weeds in the shopping precinct (Spratt et al., 1998: p31). Thus, when a chance to get involved in outdoor education activities arises, they may have misconceptions. Research has suggested that many young women are also discouraged by their perceptions of the outdoors as being uncomfortable and potentially dangerous (Mason, 1995); where one has to wear 'uncool' clothes (McCormack and Spratt, 1996); whilst contending with a macho, hostile environment (Spratt et al., 1998) and all this in a gendered space (Rose, 1993). In addition, the current fashion is for short bouts of activity that give an adrenaline rush as opposed to the more sustained involvement generally required in many outdoor activities (Mason, 1995).

The social status of young women may also block participation. There is often a cost implication, sometimes actual, sometimes hidden, which may mediate against young people particularly from a working class background (Mason, 1995: p81). In addition, traditionally it has been the role of women to support the leisure activities of men (Thompson, 1990: p135). In some families, young women have responsibility for caring for younger siblings (Spence, 1990). Dodd (1990) also describes the matriarchal figure in many working class families. The matriarch may give permission to break with tradition, allowing a daughter to get involved in an outdoor education experience, or she may constrain the daughter. Young women's perceptions and previous negative experiences of the outdoors may compound their reticence in demanding involvement in outdoor education activities.

To overcome some of these blocks, many outdoor educators are moving away from traditional outdoor education with its central theme of a physical interaction with the outdoors. A recent residential for inner-city young women involved balancing high ropes, archery and shelter building, with environmental sculpture, story telling, 'let's go and explore' the grounds of the centre, and poetry writing. Consequently, the less physical young women had activities in which they could excel. Conversations ranged from environmental awareness, relationships and ethical issues through to spiritual issues. In this setting, Maria was able to excel in the more creative activities...and the young women who had tackled high ropes with accomplishment were also able to recognise their creative or interpersonal skills.

A recurring debate is whether gender-specific outdoor education experiences should be encouraged. Henderson (1999: p247) argues in favour of these, and includes all-male groups in this category. She states that people and, in this case, young people, must have access to choice. However, evidence suggests that in a mixed setting, particularly one in which there is the potential for physical prowess, males tend to dominate, creating a competitive atmosphere, promoting male superiority (Scraton, 1986; and Humberstone, 1984). Yet, Scraton (1992), also notes that young women often develop their identity as women through their relationships with boys and young men. Meanwhile, Lynch (1999: p258) argues against gender-specific work, highlighting the role that outdoor education can play in promoting and demonstrating inclusion and integration. For Baker-Graham (1999: p72) the critical validation for promoting work with young women, must be the clarity of intended outcomes. She explains that many young women have 'internalised a 'secondary citizen' complex'. It may be through being in a single-gender group, that young women can challenge these stereotypes.

For Maria, at this particular time, being a member of a young women's outdoor experience was important. She was away from the taunts of young men, and from the competitive environment she feared they might create. It would appear that outdoor educators must provide varied opportunities, in terms of group structure, activities, purpose and intended outcomes, if outdoor education is to be truly accessible:

> *I probably wouldn't have gone if it was mixed. On the high ropes you would have got put off if there were boys...most of the boys would have taken over...and the boys (from another group) did on the pool and the table tennis. If we'd been chatting, boys would have been listening in and we wouldn't have been able to talk about the same things. The environment was cool...if there had been boys, they would have chatted through and they wouldn't have heard what we had to do...they might have made fun.* (Charlotte, 11)

Leadership with Young Men

As Ogilvie (1993: p112) rightly points out 'from birth, boys are bombarded by a set of attitudes which anachronistically hark back to the values of those times when food had to be hunted and territory or possessions defended'. Despite living in what many people would see as more enlightened times there is still a very strong undercurrent of masculine values which permeate every aspect of the upbringing of young men. Finding their place in the peer group pecking order still tends to revolve around physical prowess whilst attitudes such as 'boys don't cry' and 'stand up for yourself' remain the dominant influence on boys and young men. The compulsion to meet these exacting standards means that even for boys and young men with strong personalities the peer group norms and mores of behaviour need to be met, in public at least.

This attitude has, however, led to rising difficulties in coping on an emotional level for young men: the notable rise in young male suicides being just the most obvious example of young men not being able to cope. Ironically the very culture and values which young men are encouraged to adopt is the reason why they are increasingly struggling to cope with the pressures of a modern society that does not depend on physical ability or masculine attributes. This is further compounded, as Eric Maddern (2000: p137), says because:

> ...not only are boys falling behind girls in most aspects of education, but there are also fewer traditional male work roles, so many young men are faced with uncertain job futures. They are surrounded by consumer desirables and a culture that measures worth by material possessions. Unable to legitimately acquire these symbols of value there is a build up of frustration and anger which eventually either explodes or implodes. If fuelled by hanging out in street gangs it may come out in manic aggression, violence, delinquency and crime...or if suffered alone this pent up emotion will be turned inward and result in a downward spiral of despair, the end result of which is all too often suicide...and of course, alcohol, drugs (and for some, cyberspace) often provide a ready escape route from life's hard realities...as a result of all this many young men, charged up with anger or anxiety, are accidents waiting to happen.

Maddern goes on to suggest that young men rarely feel truly valued and gives the example of teenage mothers and whether they should give up their child for adoption with the young father rarely being mentioned or considered. It might seem as if this view of young men points an excessively bleak picture and Maddern is quick to admit that there are many young men who have very successful and fulfilling lives. It is, however, true that many of the difficulties associated with youth are seen as typically male issues and this is amplified by a mass media which seems keen to put forward the 'laddish' culture as a phenomenon of modern society. This culture even seems to be encouraged by the repeated 'dumbing down' of many prime time television and radio shows aimed at young people.

It is against this difficult background that the leader working with young men has to achieve something positive and worthwhile. As with any other group of young people it is inappropriate to attempt to transfer the values and beliefs of an adult leader onto the young people. Taking a group of young unemployed men to an opera, to take an extreme example, might seem like a wonderful idea to a well educated, middle class leader but would be unlikely to endear him to the young men in question. However, it would also be inappropriate for the leader to adopt the 'laddish' culture exhibited by those in their charge. Not only would this also be likely to backfire but it is this very culture that is standing in the way of the work of the leader. In Chapters

2, 3, 4 and 8 it was discussed how openness and honesty were critical components of a worthwhile learning and personal development experience. It was also suggested, in Chapter 1, that one of the significant roles of a leader is to help young people through a difficult period of questioning and exploration as they move into adulthood. A culture, such as that often displayed by young men, which mandates that expressions of emotions or feelings, much less the discussion of private and personal issues, are somehow 'weak' and not to be tolerated obviously stands in the way of this work.

Maddern suggests that one of the solutions to this difficulty is the re-introduction of traditional 'rites of passage' found in many so-called 'primitive' societies and he has done a great deal of useful work in this direction at Cae Mabon, the 'village encampment' he has founded in Wales. He writes (2000: p143) that:

> *We live in exciting, but dangerous times...society is being unpicked from below by a chronic lack of heart, particularly in the downcast and the young...If we are to reweave the web we need to spend more time and effort with our youth. We need the growth of people to be higher in value than the growth of material wealth. At the moment there is something desperately missing in the way that we bring up our children...the special challenge is to work with those who are in the testing time of moving from childhood dependency to being self-reliant, inter-dependant, creative, active adults. We believe that the rites of passage perspective adds invaluable potency to this work, and ultimately not just for disadvantaged youth, but for all.*

How does this transfer to the leader working with young men? This book is focused on the immediate, day-to-day, work of leaders working with young people rather than policies and structures: given this it is initially hard to see how Eric Maddern's ideas can be put into practice. It is notable, however, that there is a significant 'rites of passage' ritual enacted with the majority of young women which revolves around the onset of puberty and the menstrual cycle. As part of this young women are encouraged, usually in all female groups, to discuss their emotions, feelings and changing physical needs as well as their aspirations for the future. Given the lack of an obvious physical 'hook' there is rarely any such equivalent programme for young men. Ogilvie (1993: p112) suggests that there:

> *...is the need for male leaders to devote more time to getting across to boys that 'being a man' does not mean acting out all those behaviours that our culture has indoctrinated males into believing are the socially approved ways to behave.*

It seems truly ironic that if the leader of young men is to put Maddern's and Ogilvie's ideas into practice than a large part of what they will be doing is trying to reverse much of the socialisation that has already taken place with young men. Whether this is done in a formalised 'rites of passage' setting or as part of an ongoing relationship and programme, it is important that the leader of young men constantly strives to show that the traditional use of macho posturing and adversarial tactics is not only immature but ultimately inefficient and counterproductive. Ogilvie (1993: p113) suggests the following game as being insightful:

> *Place a group of boys in a circle facing inward with their arms linked tightly together. Then ask the one boy you have kept out of it to try to get into the circle by any means he can devise. The resulting spectacle is usually illuminating. It usually becomes a violent attack/defend test of brute force. Rarely does the outsider resort to subtler methods. Positive, straight tactics such as a civil request or an appeal to friends are never given a thought.*

Another key consideration when working with young men is to consider the orientation (Chapter 3 Action centred leadership) and style (Chapter 2 Leadership styles) that you adopt. It is important that the use of autocratic or confrontational styles is avoided wherever possible and likewise there should also be an avoidance of appearing overly task oriented. The aim of much of the work with young people is to encourage, through facilitation, open discussion, honest dialogue and full participation. Nowhere is this more important than when working with young men.

Groups with Special Needs or Disabilities: *Phil Woodyer*

Much of what is involved in leadership is generic and applies to all activities and differing groups but when working with groups who have special needs or disabilities there are particular skills required and particular knowledge of groups and individuals. As with all groups but perhaps more so with these groups, what is required is a vast amount of sensitivity to the young person's needs and a vast amount of patience. In no circumstances should the difficulties of working with special needs' groups and groups with disabilities be used as an excuse for not doing things. There are additional leadership issues involved but as long as these are treated with intelligence and sensitivity, working with these groups can be a very rewarding and life-enhancing experience.

A leader needs to know all the important things that may affect an individual's participation in the activities and how to relate to and communicate with them. For example someone may have a colostomy bag: how will this affect the fitting of equipment or how this person may be moved or handled? In the case of epilepsy, what conditions may precipitate a fit and how can this risk be reduced or removed without restricting the activity? With special needs' groups there will be increased leader and carer to young people ratios and there will need to be much more reliance placed on group leaders and carers to help and to communicate with group members. This communication is to enhance that between the leader and the group members not to replace it. A leader should never make the mistake of talking always to carers rather than to the young people.

Activity briefings may be meaningless to some special needs' groups without special interpretation from the groups' leaders or carers, so although the briefing may be to the whole group it may only be understood by some group members or may be mainly for the benefit of the leaders.

Learning difficulties

Groups with learning difficulties may not always react in ways that seem logical. They may have the normal fears associated with activities like fear of heights, fear of enclosed spaces, fear of water, but in addition they may also be afraid of the equipment or afraid of the leader. It is therefore important to be aware and sympathetic and, with the group leaders, build up the trust necessary for doing the activities together.

Some with learning difficulties can be the opposite to those mentioned above and have no concept of fear. They need to be observed closely or they may throw themselves into things or off things before they have been fitted with the correct safety equipment or been given the correct briefing.

Often groups with learning difficulties may not be very strong or have a great deal of endurance so it is important not to over-face them with activities which are too hard or too long. One of the main reasons for doing activities with special needs' groups is to build up their confidence by enabling them to succeed at things they did not think they could do; so achievement at whatever level is very important for these groups.

One exception to the lack of physical strength are those with Down's syndrome who can be very strong as you may find out if you are grabbed by such a person; where safety is involved the leader may need a back up.

Some members of these groups tend to get cold very quickly and should not be kept in cold water or in a wet condition for a long time.

With these groups, the simpler the better; not too many instructions at once; clear, concise, verbal instructions, illustrated if possible, kept to a minimum and relevant to safety matters. These instructions may have to be repeated many times but this is not a problem and the more fun it can be made the more easily group members will remember. There will be varying special needs within one group but the group leaders should be aware if the briefing is being pitched at the right level.

Sight impairment

This can vary from those with no vision to those who can see shadows or those with a limited range of vision. For these groups the main input is through the other senses so when describing equipment, for example, it is important to let the group members feel the items of equipment they may be using. Verbal instructions will be understood but examples cannot be illustrated by looking at things.

In order to maximise the experience it is important to highlight the other senses involved in the activity. For example, in a cave, people with a sight impairment can appreciate the sounds of the water and the acoustics of the empty passages; in boats they enjoy touching the water, the sounds of the water lapping on the sides of the boat and the wind in their face. They can be encouraged to play a full part in paddling in canoes and rafts or crewing in a sailing boat. It is important to realise that walking on uneven ground may be very difficult when sight is impaired. People with sight impairment can participate in most activities but may need to hold on to someone or to each other whilst participating.

There is a tremendous amount of trust put in a leader by people who can't see so it is important to talk in a calm and reassuring way. It is also beneficial to try activities, such as abseiling, whilst wearing a blindfold so that as a leader you can appreciate the amount of trust this person is putting in you.

Hearing impairment

Again there may be a range of hearing loss within a group and some may be able to hear and understand a group briefing if they are wearing hearing aids. It is important when talking to groups with hearing impairments for a leader to face the group so that all the individuals can see their mouth and read their lips. If the group use sign language a signer may be next to the leader for the group briefing but again it is important for a leader to communicate with group members not to the signer. It is always appreciated if the leader has some knowledge of sign language even if it is only to be able to say hello and who they are. Whenever giving instructions connected with safety it is important to emphasise points so they are fully understood and to make use of visual interpretation. This applies to any group but it is particularly important for those with hearing impairments.

It is important to set limits to areas of safe operation for these groups because they cannot be called back if they go too far and it may be too late to run after them to stop them going into a dangerous area. It is important to keep groups with hearing impairments in sight of the leader or the group's leaders and carers. Ground rules must be established beforehand and guidelines given on where to stop and where not to go. Shouting after a group with hearing impairments is a complete waste of time. They will only respond to hand signals and chasing after them could be disastrous.

Some of those with hearing impairments may wear hearing aids but these are of varying use and you cannot assume that someone with a hearing aid will hear the same as a normal hearing person. Also, hearing aids do not work if they get wet so in any activity where there is a chance of getting wet they cannot be worn.

Emotional or behavioural difficulties

Often the first problem with this kind of group is the building of trust. They can be less likely to have faith in what the leader is saying. It is important to be calm and clear when giving instructions but not too authoritarian. The group members may be very unpredictable in all situations so it is important to have a high ratio of leaders or carers to individuals and to keep a close eye on group members at all times. They may put themselves in dangerous situations for illogical reasons. It is important that group leaders are in close contact with group members who are most likely to be a problem and also to try to anticipate what might be problem areas and neutralise these before they occur. It is also important to keep an eye on safety equipment that may be tampered with.

Group members with this type of difficulty should have no problem understanding a group briefing but they may have problems in listening or in concentrating on what is being said. They may be easily distracted by what other group members are doing. It is important not to be personally affronted by what appears to be rudeness. Try to make the briefings as interesting as possible. They should not be too long and should emphasise safety elements. There may need to be an agreement that group members do not take part in the activity unless they abide by all the safety rules.

Ambulant difficulties and wheelchair users

Group members with ambulant problems are well aware of all the restrictions on what they can do; this is something they do not need reminding of. What they need is encouragement and help to do as much as they can. Briefings should be positive, not negative. It may be better to sit down and discuss things with the group rather than stand over them, emphasising their disability. When discussing how to do things it is important to talk or communicate with the person with the disability rather than talking over them always to the group leader.

People with ambulant problems, particularly those in wheelchairs, will spend a great proportion of their time sitting doing nothing so it is important to try not to have the same scenario when they are doing activities. Even if they are not actively involved in the activity the whole time they can be involved in helping and encouraging other group members.

It is important to make sure that this type of group has enough warm and waterproof clothing for those inactive times and that if there is a chance of getting wet, they have a complete change of clothes and somewhere private to change.

It is also important to make sure when fitting clothing or equipment that it is securely fastened and not uncomfortable or likely to rub and cause sores. Those with spina bifida, for example, have little or no feeling in their legs and would not be able to tell if the leg loops on a harness was rubbing. For any assistance in moving or handling this type of individual it is usually better to take the lead from the person themselves and their leaders and carers. For any water sports it is important to make sure the individuals are safe and comfortable in any craft being used and that every person could be safely retrieved from the water if necessary.

Others

There are many other special needs that require individual special attention e.g. those with limbs missing, hydrocephalus, brittle bones or cystic fibrosis. In most cases group leaders will be able to enlighten leaders on any special information required when working with these individuals. With groups or individuals who have diabetes the session should not be too long or tiring without the opportunity to rest and eat. Only some of the individuals concerned will be able to monitor their own condition and be aware of any danger signals. Those who are prone to epilepsy will normally be controlled with drugs but leaders should be aware of any situations that could trigger a fit. This could be fatigue or stress and the leader should always be able to reach a person who is prone to epilepsy and to be able to make them safe and comfortable if they are having a fit.

Often with special needs groups it is difficult to obtain equipment that fits properly. Although we may have to improvise when getting equipment to fit it should be done in a manner that does everything possible to maintain the dignity of the individual. There are some distinct examples where consideration will need to be given to clothing and equipment:

- People in wheelchairs are often overweight and will need large sizes in cagoules etc.
- Those with Down's syndrome also tend to be large in the body although they may be quite short. People with hydrocephalus have extra large heads and will therefore need extra large helmets.
- If using helmets for activities it is important to ensure that the helmet fits properly and will not fall over the eyes.
- Sometimes equipment may be inappropriate. For example if an individual has their own specially fitting shoes it is usually better to let them wear these than to try to squeeze them into a standard boot or wellington.

There are now items of equipment which have been specially made for those with special needs. The Tools for Living Department at Brunel University has developed equipment such as the Kite Harness which can be used for abseiling with individuals who use a wheelchair. The Fish Buoyancy Aid has been designed to fit those whose bodies are not a standard shape and they are very versatile in use with people with disabilities. If any of this specialised equipment is being used it is important to be completely familiar with the methods for putting it on and using it, before using it with group members.

Apart from the specialised equipment, people working with special needs' groups have produced much modified and adapted equipment. For example, extra pieces of tape can be used for modifying sports equipment and outdoor gear; clothing and buoyancy aids can be used for padding and support for people sitting in boats.

Challenging Young People: *Abi Paterson*

The title of this contribution makes me cringe and smile simultaneously. 'Challenging' is the current euphemism for anti-social, violent, drug taking...and I cringe. I smile when I think of challenges we can encourage young people to take on, to move towards their potential, to make choices for themselves, to take control of their lives.

Who are we talking about?

Most people try illegal drugs, drink alcohol illegally, have an occasion of unsafe sex, break the law, etc., at some stage in their lives. For most of us there will be no lasting effect on the rest of our lives or long-term consequence. For others the reverse will be true. Youth at risk, troubled youth, disaffected, disadvantaged, disengaged young people are those whose behaviour and activities have placed them at risk of negative long-term consequences such as physical or mental health issues perhaps through drug taking or self-harm; a criminal record that cannot be deemed as spent; or they are experiencing the consequences of their behaviour in other ways, they have been thrown out of home or decided to leave, have become a young parent, or have become a target; and perhaps most importantly they have become alienated from or are in the process of becoming alienated from some or all of the formal support structures available to them.

How do I work with these people?

The principles of working well with people are pretty constant and apply equally to challenging young people:

- I work with people as individuals—albeit within a group.
- I develop trust between each individual young person and me.
- I develop a sense of belonging and ownership within each person.
- I start from where each person is.
- I work with activities that excite the individuals: when did you last go to something in your spare time that had nothing in it for you?
- I treat individuals as adults: people hate being treated like children.
- I establish clear well defined boundaries that the people have a real part in creating.
- I give real responsibility and real decision making control to people.
- I create a place that feels safe—for young people this often means out of school.
- Step by step—**FUN, FUN, FUN.**

Essentially, I aim to work with honesty, charisma, and integrity, and I find to do it well I have to be really clear headed as well.

Models and theories

Theories and models are simplifications that enable us to understand the complexity of the real world—they are only useful so long as they do that. The theories that I have found to be useful in my work with people are those that expand our concept of what intelligence is, allow for individuals to differ from each other, particularly in the way that we process information and learn. I like Neuro-Linguistic Programming (NLP) and the concept of multiple intelligences as a means of understanding how I process information. I like reality therapy as a way of understanding my behaviour and I like the development-training model of experiential learning as a means of changing myself. I strongly recommend that you look up and read about these and other related developmental theories. (See Lawlor and Handley, 1996; and Wubbolding and Brickell, 1999 for more information.)

Reality therapy suggests that people develop behaviour patterns to meet their core personal needs. These patterns may be less than successful and be positively damaging, particularly over time when the original purpose is lost. A classic example would be a young person who is bored, sees that the boredom can be solved by joyriding and may end up in hospital or incarcerated, both of which are potentially rather boring, but once in prison loses sight of the original purpose of joyriding and continues with crime. Similarly, a young person may have no control over parts of their life and the things that happen to them which are painful. One solution is to take control of their pain through some form of self-harm. This may solve the control issues for that person *and* has the potential for long-term consequences.

These solutions to core needs become established in an individual over a long period of time. There are no rules about how long change will take. I have seen a young person rapidly change their life from being a homeless drug addict, to clean with a flat, partner and job, within months of joining a project. And lose it all weeks later. Sometimes people change their behaviour dramatically over the period of an intensive course and become most trusted and relied upon: and revert to their anti-social behaviour, only worse, just as the course ends...it is as if they cannot believe they can be different, cannot take the change home. Change can be rapid or slow; another part of the NLP/reality therapy models explores self-perception (Figure 23).

If the core shape in this model is how I see myself, the chances are that a change that is close to this perception is probably possible to sustain: it is easy to expand my self-perception to

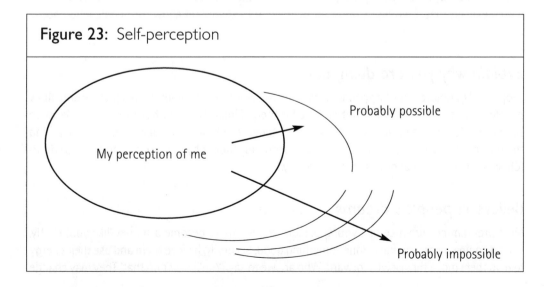

Figure 23: Self-perception

Probably possible

My perception of me

Probably impossible

include it. In contrast a large change is way outside my understanding of myself and probably difficult to sustain. I can however, take short steps over time to reach a substantial and sustainable change.

What does all this mean in practice? There are few absolute rules about working with challenging young people. There are a few top tips!

Constantly develop yourself

Personal development does not have an end point. Believe in what you are doing, on occasion tell young people about parts of your development and you will be credible.

Walk the talk

This is the actions speak louder than words principle. If people can see you using the principles to develop yourself effectively, they are more likely to take them on themselves. Fail to do this and people will see straight through you. Particularly remember to keep developing your emotional understanding, it's absolutely crucial for working with people.

Always give real choice

Voluntary attendance is central to effective work, particularly with challenging young people. The choice must be a real choice. 'Attend or go down' is *not* a place to start developing good decision making. It isn't a choice. Once attending, all activities must be voluntary; encourage, suggest, discuss, offer solutions...remember you are enabling someone to understand themselves better.

Individual development

The only person who always needs to understand what has happened to me is me. You do not need to know what I have learned unless it is helpful to me to tell you. Working with individuals in a group usually involves people exploring their experiences together as a way of understanding better, explain that it would be good for everybody to share and allow for people who choose not to.

Explain why you are doing things

People will get more out of anything if they see the point of it. Explain the big picture and allow people time to explore what might be in it for them. Similarly, if you have to ask people to do something, for example, wear seat belts or stick together, explain the reason why you are asking them to do it. If you can't think of a good reason, question why you are asking them to do it! (Check with your manager or insurance policy.)

Believe in people's dreams

Most programmes produce one young person who wants to become a trainer 'like you'. Firstly, what a complement: you have done something good. Secondly, believe them and use their energy to help them move themselves forward. Who are we to say, 'You'll never do that'. They may change or as they develop the dream may change. The dreams are what move us forward. The old quote applies 'whether you think you can or whether you think you can't you are probably right'.

Small changes — long-term development

One of the transfer difficulties of activity residential programmes is that people then have to go home and work out how to manifest the behaviour change amongst different people. The more substantial the change the less likely it is that people at home will accept the 'new me'. It is too far outside their perception of me. Small changes that I can 'practice' at home are more likely to be effective. However, there remains a place for intensive residential work and many organisations that do this are now coaching transfer-to-home understanding from the start of the course and insisting on a partnership with an organisation back at the young person's home to continue the work.

Avoid confrontation

Nothing mushrooms a situation faster than 'chesting up' to an angry young person. Calmly entering into a conversation or engaging in activity will usually defuse a situation. Remember to acknowledge that you have heard. Very, very rarely appearing to be angry will have a positive response: use carefully.

Give people the opportunity to change

Treat all people with the utmost respect and trust: and prove to them how, for example, trustworthy they are by keeping all valuables carefully. Real trust takes time and step-by-step experiences to grow. You can front-load situations by explaining, 'other groups in the past have had belongings go missing. I know you can be trusted and that nothing like that will happen with this group'.

Use your intuition

Your intuition is probably information that you have stored subconsciously. It is therefore probably a very powerful tool. Explore and use it.

When all else fails — give up

This is another tool that I have found useful and need not be saved until last. It basically involves explaining to a young person that you do not know what to do next—you have no idea how to move forward and that you need their help. This metaphorically puts the ball back in their court and potentially re-engages them with the consequences of their own behaviour and encourages them to create a way forward, which you must be prepared to accept. Be prepared for a long discussion about the effects of their behaviour on you or a short 'dun no' and a shrug!

Personal and social skills development

There are dozens of effective media for personal development; drama, art, and football, cooking, developing and running your own business. All have their part to play in development and have their own strengths. Adventurous activity is another medium with its own strengths and weaknesses. It is the development of self-esteem, self-confidence, self-awareness, personal and social skills and life skills, etc. that are the real curricula of our work.

I have found it extremely hard to document years of experience into 2,000 words. It tells less than half the story, gives little of the full picture. Experience builds understanding and myriad of methods, strategies and tools. My advice is get out there and do it. If you're looking for a good place to start try Fairbridge.

Working with Young People from Ethnic Communities: *Judy Ling Wong*

> *I do not feel that I know enough about this, but I feel that it is important. Would you help me to know a little bit more?*

To be able to ask such a question with interest and care is an indication of a high level of confidence and skill in relating successfully to young people from different ethnic communities. It is essential to establish meaningful contact, and to be open to the specific information a young person can give, against an awareness of the different settings from which difference is played out. Programmes of activity need to be designed to reflect the needs and concerns of the many social and cultural backgrounds of the young people concerned. Anyone working with young people from ethnic communities needs training to gain the awareness and skills to effectively nurture and bring forward their unique individual contribution as who they are.

Young people belonging to the immigrant generation have specific needs around loss, culture clash, language difficulties and social isolation. It is particularly important to include elements of their culture of origin so that the inevitable introduction to what is new takes place against some anchors of familiarity. An effort should be made to ensure that any family members understand and approve of the programmes of activity offered.

Young people, from ethnic communities, who are born here, are bicultural if not multicultural. They are British, with a special cultural relationship to their country of origin. There is a need to attend to both elements of identity. As British young people they should lay claim to all that this country offers, but this is constantly undermined by the reality of racism. The pressure this puts on the already enormous task of negotiating identity against multiple cultural backgrounds means that support is much needed.

Some of the needs and concerns named by young people from ethnic communities and their youth workers include:

- Access to leisure and sports opportunities.
- Various areas of activity perceived as the preserve of particular social groups and not open to everyone.
- Lack of gender-specific activities and events in particular for young people where religion is an important factor.
- Language is an obstacle for some but in particular for refugee communities.
- Disillusionment with authoritative institutions such as the local authority, the police and the national government.
- Decisions being made about local matters without consultation of young people, who have significant knowledge of their locality.

- Community safety, crime and young persons as victims of crime.
- Unemployment.
- Access to educational and training opportunities.
- Racism and other prejudice from other members of the local community.
- Lack of ability to be independent from family.

Some of the needs and concerns named by ethnic community groups working with their young people include:

- Under-resource of programmes of activities for young people against a scenario of competing needs on many fronts.
- Lack of public transport and other affordable transport in relation to the provision of programmes of activities.
- Lack of equipment such as basic outdoor clothes or sports kit.
- Lack of role models.
- Legacy of exclusion resulting in the lack of participation by young people in many areas of activity and a sense of powerlessness to affect change.

We have arrived in an era in which human rights, equal opportunities, access and social inclusion are on everyone's tongue. Funders are structuring their schemes to resource initiatives focused on these themes. We are poised to move significantly into action. In an increasingly multicultural society within a globalised world, young people from ethnic communities have a special contribution to make if we provide them with the support that they need. Although too many young people from ethnic communities have more than their fair share of the burden of growing up, when the right conditions are provided their energies, once directed, can be a powerhouse for action.

In any sector, in order to put a framework for full participation by young people from ethnic communities into place, there is a need for organisational development underpinned by a senior level commitment to equal opportunities and development of a strategy to enable full participation by young people from ethnic communities, including:

- Outreach to organisations working with young people from ethnic communities, including ethnic community groups.
- Consultation with young people from ethnic communities.
- Focused initiatives, in partnership with organisations working with young people from ethnic communities, including ethnic community groups.
- Use of positive images in communication and resource materials.
- Development of socially and culturally relevant range of activities.
- Allocation of staff time and resources.
- Structured staff training and development.
- Evaluation using measures which recognise that 'Equal opportunities means equal outcomes.'

Let us invest in the future of young people from ethnic communities. Our young people are our future. All of them.

Chapter 11

Leading Young People Outdoors

By leading young people outdoors we are talking about the range of activities collectively known as outdoor education or outdoor activities. The first, outdoor education implies that the activity is a second priority to the personal learning involved, for example, and in simple terms, rock climbing might be used to teach perseverance whilst rafting might be used to teach teamwork. Outdoor activities implies that the activity is being engaged in as a sport in its own right. Both outdoor education and outdoor activities have long and significant histories in Great Britain which has often led the way in the use and enjoyment of wilderness and the 'great outdoors'. Unfortunately, in recent years, a great deal of the best about being in the outdoors has been tarnished by a rising tide of legislation and fears about litigation. There is also an increasing aversion to risk in society in general which has meant that many outdoor activities with young people have become so constrained as to lose any true meaning. In essence both outdoor education and outdoor activities have a relationship with risk that puts them apart from other activities with young people. Despite these issues with risk the continuing popularity of the outdoors as a learning medium with young people means that many leaders will be involved with it in some way at some stage in their work.

This chapter can, of necessity, only be an introduction to this vast and fascinating subject: however, it can serve two purposes. Firstly for those leaders who are already involved with leading young people outdoors it summarises some of the main theories associated with risk and the deliberate use of risk, whilst for non-outdoor leaders who may be accompanying groups it gives them an understanding of the nature of risk. This chapter should be read together with Chapter 14 Rules, Roles and Responsibility to give an understanding of who is responsible for what in the outdoors.

The Outdoors as a Learning Medium

Leading young people outdoors has its own unique advantages and disadvantages as well as its own unique power and difficulties. The most notable of the advantages when leading young people outdoors is that it is a powerful and novel learning medium. In addition to the other learning factors discussed in Chapter 8 the outdoors is generally reckoned to be a particularly powerful learning medium because:

The outdoors is an alien experience

For most young people outdoor activities will be new and different to their everyday experiences. Some activities, such as caving, may be extremely so. This disorientation means that people are very receptive to learning as they have few references to past experience to help them.

The outdoors is an equaliser

This manifests itself in a number of ways from a young offender realising that they have as much to offer as other members of their group, to a manager realising that their secretary has hidden strengths that they themselves do not possess. With regard to young people in particular the outdoors can be an equaliser in a number of ways not least because it does not depend on simple strength or physical ability to succeed.

Real consequences can be used as learning points

It is very hard in hypothetical classroom situations to get people to accept the true consequences of their actions whereas in the outdoor environment every action has a good or bad consequence some of which can be unpleasant or uncomfortable, getting wet or cold for example.

Fears and challenges can be approached in a supportive environment

Although a young person might be very conscious of losing face in a home environment, in the outdoors where most of their fellow group members are experiencing the same fears and concerns it is easier to be open about them. This is amplified by the natural bonding and mutual support that working together in the outdoors engenders.

The outdoors is fun

This is an element often missed by people but it is a simple fact that people learn quickly if they are enjoying themselves.

Everyday concerns are left behind

Learning can be a difficult experience when everyday concerns such as home and school issues are constantly at the back of a young person's mind. By transferring the learning to the outdoor environment and thus detaching it from the 'real world' these concerns can be left behind.

Emotions are heightened

In everyday life many young people, especially young men, tend to keep a tight rein on their emotions which usually acts as a strong barrier to any form of personal development. Outdoor activities bring emotions, both good and bad, to the surface enabling them to be experienced, shared and built on.

Communication is enhanced

There is very little as effective as powerful shared experiences when trying to open up meaningful conversation. The powerful emotions and levelling of group members engendered by the outdoor experience means that conversation is often carried out at the 'feelings and emotions' level rather than the more normal 'cocktail' levels (see Chapter 4 The levels of communication).

The very nature of the outdoors and outdoor activities means that powerful and highly memorable moments are experienced

These moments mean that not only will an experience be remembered for a long time but perception and with it, learning, is increased to an elevated level (see Chapter 13 What is Success?).

Although there has been a move away from doing activities with a high emotional impact, the outdoors still represents an almost unique vehicle for personal and group development. It is important to note, however, that any learning and development is discussed and reviewed (see Chapters 8 Learning, and 9 Reviewing and Feedback) in order to bring out the true benefits of the experience. It is also important to be aware that powerful experiences and emotions, such as those engendered in the outdoors need careful handling. In recent years there has been a greater realisation that whilst the physical risk to people on outdoor activities and education has been increasingly minimised the risk of psychological harm has often been neglected. Psychological harm, or trauma, is just as real when considering outdoor activities and can even, in some cases, have longer lasting effects. Most aspects of physical harm can also be applied to psychological harm. It is important, therefore, that emotions are not raised which cannot, afterwards, be resolved.

The Question of Risk

Risk is a central part of the outdoor learning experience for two completely different reasons. Firstly, it forms an ever-present backdrop to almost all outdoor activities; it introduces the question of safety and the minimising of risk to acceptable levels. Secondly, it is the element of risk that not only gives many outdoor activities their excitement but also their potential for use in self-development. This section looks at risk from both of these viewpoints. It explains how risk is defined and quantified and then looks at how risk is individual and different for different people.

On safety

Whilst this chapter does not set out to be a comprehensive work on safety in the outdoors (there are many good books on the subject), risk and safety cannot be separated. There are a large number of factors which contribute to safe practice, notably:

- attitude of mind
- ethos
- responsibility
- procedures; formal and informal
- legislation
- equipment
- leadership

Of these perhaps the most important is attitude of mind coupled with good leadership. All the other factors are, to some extent, features of the physical practice of an outdoor centre or organisation, the attitude of the outdoor staff, however, is not only less tangible but also less influenced by external factors. Whilst bad procedures, bad equipment, and so on can all be overcome by good, conscientious staff the opposite is not true. The best system using the best equipment will still be unsafe if the person in charge doesn't care about safety. It is important that if you are accompanying, rather than leading, a group of young people on an outdoor activity session that you are happy with the safety procedures and, in particular, the outdoor staff. Almost all local authorities will have a set of operating procedures that must be adhered to when taking young people on outdoor or residential trips. These are worth investigating and adhering to even if your trip is not under the auspices of the local authority. You should also be aware of the *Activity Centres (Young Persons' Safety) Act 1995*. This act which is operated through the 'Adventure Activities Licensing Regulations 1996' and by the 'Adventure Activities Licensing Authority' (AALA) means that all commercial providers of specified outdoor activities must have been inspected and licensed. In essence if a leader takes people under the age of eighteen on most outdoor activities in return for payment then the chances are that these regulations will apply to them, or, more likely, their employer. To operate without a license is a criminal offence. A client, or potential client, has the right, if this legislation applies, to inspect the license of an outdoor provider.

Before risk can be defined it must be understood that there are two fundamentally different types of risk associated with outdoor activities. These are 'perceived risk' and 'actual risk'. Perceived risk is what the person involved in an activity feels the risk to be whilst actual risk is the risk that is present in reality. With most novices in the outdoors the perceived risk will usually be much higher than the actual risk because they will find it difficult to make the logical leap of faith that such a thing as rock climbing is actually very safe if managed properly. It is perceived risk that outdoor education utilises as a learning tool, the actual risk involved is often very low. It is wise, however, not to forget that perceived risk feels like actual risk to the person involved and should not, therefore be discounted or treated with contempt.

Bearing this distinction in mind, risk is best defined (Wharton, 1996) as being the:

Likelihood of harm occurring multiplied by the probable severity of that harm.

To take an example of this, using an arbitrary scale of ten, rock climbing in a normal outdoor centre setting can be seen to be low risk:

$$\text{Risk in rock climbing} = 1 \times 9 = 9$$

This is because whilst the severity of the harm that might occur is high (9) a person might die, the actual likelihood of that harm occurring is very low (1).

Ghyll scrambling, or gorge walking, on the other hand is a much higher risk:

$$\text{Risk from ghyll scrambling} = 4 \times 6 = 24$$

This occurs because, even though the likely harm that might happen to a student is somewhat lower (4) the likelihood of that harm occurring is much higher (6) giving a higher total risk. In other words the activity that seems safer is actually the more dangerous one. This is not at all unusual in the outdoor world, think of the so-called low level activities often used with younger children such as assault courses or mountain biking. Whilst they might seem safe they are in reality more risky than kayaking, caving or rock climbing where much more direct control is exercised by the outdoor staff.

This difference between the actual risk and the perceived risk is important to the leader of young people because it enables risk to be put into perspective. Using the examples above it might be tempting to let a group of youngsters go charging off on mountain bikes because it is perceived as a low risk; when in reality it is one of the most accident prone activities in the outdoors. Incidentally, probably the highest risk element in any trip is the drive to and from the venue. Many outdoor activities are only perceived as dangerous because they are novel and outside of the direct experience of the people involved. Far greater risks, such as driving, which are encountered every day are considered to be far more acceptable by the very virtue of their being mundane.

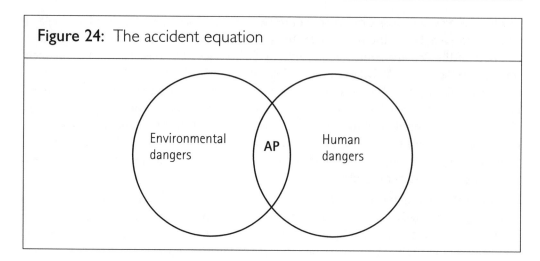

Figure 24: The accident equation

The accident equation

Another way of looking at levels of risk is to use the accident equation developed by Simon Priest (1990) and shown in Figure 24.

This makes the assumption that there is an accident potential (AP) when environmental and human elements come into contact. To give a rather glib example; a raging white water river will not harm you whilst you sit on the bank, it is when you become involved with the river, through kayaking or canoeing, that there is an accident potential. It is when the two elements, environmental and human, contain inherent dangers that the accident potential becomes greater and when there are a number of these elements that it is at its greatest.

For example, on a kayaking trip the following elements might come into play:

Environmental	Human
Rocks in river	Inexperienced paddler
Low water	Old fibreglass kayak
Bend in river	Large group

It can be seen that in this example there is a large number of possible combinations which give rise to a risky venture. Tight group control might alleviate some of the potential combinations but there are simply too many possible combinations to safely overcome in this case. The key to safety in the outdoors is often that accidents are caused by lots of little things, rather than one big thing, going wrong.

Matching the risk to the individual

One of the most important things to remember about risk is that perceived risk is different for everybody and actual risk is different for every group leader. What might be an impossibly dangerous activity for one leader might be perfectly safe for a more experienced or better qualified leader. Likewise every leader is familiar with the student who cannot be persuaded that a high rope course is perfectly safe because they perceive it as dangerous whilst other members of the group are quite happy on the same obstacles. It is the difference in perceived risk that is discussed here. The difference in actual risk is one which only experience, training and the judgement that comes with them can teach.

Remembering that one of the central components of the outdoor experience is that risk is used as a tool for self-development it follows that the level of perceived risk must be matched to the individual student for maximum effectiveness. (There is rarely any need, or justification, to increase the level of actual risk for individual students in a group situation.)

Hopkins and Putnam (1993) refer to this need as the 'problem of the match' and describe it as shown in Figure 25. This figure clearly shows that the potential for personal growth increases in line with the level of (perceived) risk until it reaches a stage where there is a dramatic fall off as the level of risk becomes too high. It is at this critical zone, where the potential for personal growth is highest, that outdoor leaders should be attempting to pitch their activities. The whole point of the problem of the match, and the reason why it is a problem, is that the match will be different for every member of a group.

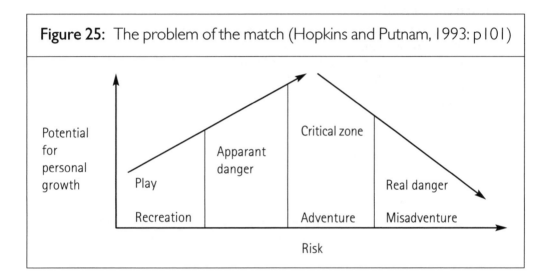

Figure 25: The problem of the match (Hopkins and Putnam, 1993: p101)

Some students may be scared of heights whilst others may be scared of water and yet others scared of the enforced sociability of the group environment. The mark of a really good outdoor leader is that they will be able to pitch various activities at various levels so that everyone in the group will operate at some stage in the 'critical zone' with only an absolute minimum being bored by spending some time in the recreation zone and even less experiencing the fear or panic of the misadventure zone. In an ideal world the whole group will constantly be moving between the adventure and critical zones throughout the duration of an outdoor course.

Those people who have done much reading about outdoor education will instantly recognise that there is little new in Hopkins and Putnam's ideas. Rather they are based on the classic four stages of adventure first developed by Colin Mortlock (1984) these can be summarised as shown in Figure 26.

In Mortlock's model, stage three, that of frontier adventure, equates with the critical zone in Figure 25. As with Hopkins and Putnam, Mortlock makes the point that these stages will be different for each individual. What may be one person's play might easily be another person's misadventure.

Figure 26: Mortlock's stages of adventure

Stage one: Play

> Working at well below normal abilities
> Minimal involvement
> Fear of physical harm is absent
> Response—range from 'fun/pleasant' to 'boring/waste of time'

Stage two: Adventure

> Feels in control but conscious of using abilities
> Fear of physical harm is virtually absent
> Progression stage/skills learning

Stage three: Frontier Adventure

> No longer in total control but able to succeed with effort/luck
> Uncertain of outcome
> Fear of physical harm and experience of psychological stress
> Pride and satisfaction on completion

Stage four: Misadventure

> Beyond control
> Fear, panic or terror
> Possible high learning situation

A feature of Mortlock's stages of adventure is that they are clearly sequential with, for example, students needing to pass through the adventure stage of skills learning before moving into the higher risk of the frontier adventure stage.

Discussion: the nature of risk

There is a philosophical element to any discussion of risk; what cannot be denied in all this, however, is that there is also a very practical element. Risk in the outdoor environment can be summed up as all that is good in outdoor education and all that is bad. When attending an outdoor course young people risk many things, some obvious and some not so obvious:

They risk physical harm, of all the risks involved in the outdoors this should be the one that a leader can best keep under control. The difficulty is that if we go to the extreme and make outdoor courses 100 per cent safe then the young people involved risk deception. We cannot make outdoor courses purely perceived risk otherwise they might just as well go to Alton Towers, the outdoors is a risky environment.

More than most things, students risk the danger of embarrassment, providing that this doesn't get out of hand it is all part of a healthy learning experience. It is always worth remembering of course, that people have very different tolerance levels when it comes to being embarrassed. A major element in embarrassment is in the risk of being vulnerable and open which is an unnatural and awkward state for most young people, but one that is essential if true learning is to take place. A very real cause for concern, however, is the potential risk of psychological harm where emotions have gone too far, someone has been genuinely terrified during an activity or badly humiliated in a review. It goes without saying that such a situation is totally unacceptable. However, psychological harm can be desperately hard to guard against, there are no safety ropes attached to a person's emotions. This is one area where all leaders need to be extra vigilant.

Many young people, if not most, will find that they might well have to risk facing up to their fears and, even more daunting for many, risk being honest with themselves and take the greatest risk of finding out something that they don't like about themselves:

> *...risks must be taken because the greatest hazard in life is to risk nothing,*
> *the person who risks nothing does nothing, has nothing, is nothing.*
> *They may avoid suffering and sorrow,*
> *but they cannot learn, feel, change, grow, love or live.*
> *Chained by their certainties they are slaves,*
> *they have forfeited their freedom.*
> *Only a person who risks is free.*   (author unknown)

As for leaders involved with taking young people into the outdoors it cannot be stressed enough that it is not something that can be taken lightly. This chapter simply highlights some of the questions about the use of risk and the power of learning that can be engendered through the outdoors: in no way does it qualify anyone to take a group of young people into the outdoors. There is a current debate happening about the validity of qualifications when compared to experience in outdoor activities. This is not a debate that need involve a leader, except philosophically, because they should feel obliged, morally if not legally, not to undertake any form of outdoor leadership without being fully competent; in qualification and experience.

Chapter 12

Looking After Yourself and Others

If you are going to be in a position of leadership with young people you also need to know how to look after yourself, as well as others. This can take many forms, some seemingly trivial and some potentially very serious. This chapter starts with a section on abuse; although some people might question why this section is in this chapter it is worth turning the question on its head for a minute. Simply put, if you always approach a questionable situation with the question 'am I doing the right thing here?' you shouldn't go too far wrong.

It is worthwhile considering however, that the 'right thing' is not always clear-cut. Priest and Gass (1997: p285) identify two different approaches, principle ethics and virtue ethics:

> Principle ethics are guided by a proactively determined set of impartial rules, often determined by a governing professional organisation or by the current professional standards of behaviour if no such guidelines exist...leaders following principle ethics examine their actions and choices, looking to the questions of 'What should I do?' and 'Is this situation un-ethical?'...Virtue ethicists, however, believe that you must examine the particular factors and influences of each act, asserting that 'correct behaviour' is determined in each specific situation and that you can not link any decision made in other situations...specifically, virtue ethics are concerned with professional character traits, focusing on the questions of 'Who shall I be?' and 'Am I doing the best for my client?'...the strengths of each approach are the very weaknesses of the other.

Principle ethics, that are drawn up as a generic code of behaviour, might well not be flexible enough to allow for individual action which would be suitable at the time. They do however ensure a consistently safe way of working for both the 'client', the young people in this case, and the leader. Virtue ethics, on the other hand, allow the leader to make decisions regarding individual situations and thereby allow them to operate to the complete limit of their effectiveness. In this case, however, the leader must be able to constantly justify their actions and be prepared to answer for their choices.

The section below sets out a series of guidelines based largely on principle ethics; this means that they tend to be very prescriptive and largely black and white. This is particularly so for the last guideline, 'follow your organisation's policies to the letter'. Whilst following a set of guidelines such as this will, therefore, allow you to work in the comparative confidence that you will not lay yourself open to accusations of misbehaviour they can be stifling. If you, as the leader, chose to follow a code of virtue ethics it may be that a guideline requiring you to follow your organisation's policies is untenable. To take an example highlighted elsewhere in this book; you know that a number of young people in your charge smoke cannabis, your organisation's policies are very clear on this, there is to be no use of illegal drugs. (See the discussion in Chapter 2 The role of leadership). You know, however, that if you enforce this policy, whether you agree with it or not, the young people involved will still smoke cannabis but will do it in secret and may get involved with crime or harder drugs. If you ignore the policy and allow the young people to smoke cannabis on the understanding that they will be open and honest about their drug use you may be able to influence the direction and actions they could take. However, if someone in authority found out they were smoking cannabis and wanted to report them, and then found out that it was with your knowledge; would you be prepared to accept responsibility? There is no easy answer and certainly not one that can be learnt from a book. Perhaps the only practical solution is to work for an organisation that is prepared to be flexible and support its staff if the need, and the justification, arises.

Allegations of Abuse and How to Avoid Them

Hopefully you will never face an accusation from, or by, a young person but if you do it is important that you know how to react. Even more importantly, perhaps, is knowing how to avoid such allegations in the first place. A common mistake would be to assume that only male leaders are vulnerable to misinterpretations of their actions. Young people may be as sensitive to sexual mixed messages from women leaders as from male leaders. It is sad, but pertinent, to consider that all leaders working with young people are susceptible to allegations of improper conduct or abuse. Even if serious allegations are not encountered it is very easy for a leader to become the victim of rumours and whispering or giggling comments, all of which can very quickly undermine any useful relationship that they may have had with the young people in their charge. There are a few common sense rules that can help avoiding getting into such a situation. It is worthwhile noting that many of these rules are simply a question of good practice and not anything that a leader should be doing over and above their normal routine.

Never flirt with young people

It may be flattering or you might think it is simply a bit of fun but the young person involved, or the young person's friends, may see it as something completely different. At the best you could end up with a young person thinking it is the start of a serious relationship whilst at the worst you could be accused of sexual mis-behaviour.

Avoid having obvious favourites

It is difficult, if not impossible, to prefer the company of some young people over others, however this should never be allowed to go to far. When asking for volunteers to demonstrate activities for example, make a point of going around the group rather than always going back to the same person. In the same vein avoid always choosing someone of the opposite sex to demonstrate activities with; you may not realise that you are doing it but the young people will quickly pick up on it.

Be aware of your body language and the use of physical contact

Physical contact can be a powerful tool when communicating with young people as can positive body language (see Chapter 4 Non-verbal communication) but they do need to be used with caution. It would be sad if we reached a stage where leaders where so concerned about misinterpretation that they became completely remote to young people and there is no reason why this should be the case. Only use appropriate physical contact, in appropriate situations, a touch on the shoulder is one thing, a full hug is another and beware of only using physical contact with the opposite gender. Ideally you and the young people you work with should be comfortable enough with each other that appropriate contact is acceptable but you should respect the situation if that is not the case.

Maintain an open door policy

This is not the same as the open door policy where staff are always available, but a policy where leaders never place themselves in a situation where they could not defend themselves against an accusation. The easiest way to do this is to ensure that when you are alone with a young person, as you may have to be, that others can see you or, at least, are within hearing range and accessible. You never want to be in a situation where it might come down to your word against a young person's. By maintaining an open door policy you are also sending a very clear signal that you will not be acting in a way inappropriate to the situation and the young person has no need to feel threatened or intimidated.

Never promise confidentiality

This can be difficult because if you are a good leader young people may well choose to confide in you on the understanding that what they say will be confidential. It is very easy, however, to quickly find yourself out of your depth and struggling to cope with more than you can manage. When a young person goes to tell you something 'in confidence' you should warn them that, if necessary, you might have to talk to someone else about the issues raised. Examples of this include a young person wanting to talk about a case of abuse where you might need to involve the correct authorities or a suicidal young person where you might need to bring in a counsellor.

Always report any incident or accusation

The very worse thing a leader who is concerned about an incident or accusation can do is keep to themselves. Even if the accusation is only in the form of whispering and giggling you should talk to your line manager who will then be forewarned by you rather than hearing stories from a third party. Keeping things to yourself could easily be misconstrued and you might well need the support of your line manager if things become more serious.

Be willing to ask for assistance

It may be that you need to ask for assistance from a leader of the opposite gender, for example if running a session where a lot of contact might be needed, such as a beginners trampoline or gymnastics session, or where you are fitting equipment such as climbing harnesses or buoyancy aids. Likewise, you might need to enter a 'private area' such as a dormitory or changing room where you need to be sensitive to other people's right to privacy. If you are unsure ask for another adult to be present, even if only as a witness.

Tell the young people what you are doing

In addition to the above don't suddenly act or do something to someone without warning them first, for example in a gymnastics session you might warn them that you will be helping them come out of a roll. Always be open and upfront about your intentions.

Know what to do in cases of suspected abuse

It is important that everyone who works with young people is aware of the signs and symptoms of abuse and knows what to do in a suspected case. This is quite an extensive area and outside of the scope of an introductory text such as this; it is far better if leaders attend a specialist training course. However, even without this training you should know what to do if you suspect a problem, either through physical signs, such as unexplained bruising; behaviour, such as unusually precocious or childish behaviour; or something that has been said to you, by the young person involved or a third party. The most important thing is to remember that you are not an expert; it is not down to you to go fishing for evidence or counselling or examining the young person involved. Neither is it appropriate to do nothing, you should always, without exception consult a senior colleague or your line manager and ensure that the appropriate procedures are followed. In addition to this you should keep an open mind and be prepared to develop a position of trust where the young person can talk openly to you if they wish to (but bear in mind confidence issues, above).

Follow your organisation's policies to the letter

Every organisation you work with should have a code of conduct. This is there to protect you as much as the young people in your charge and should be adhered to as any infringement could leave you open to accusation.

Burnout

A problem with many vocationally motivated leaders is they immerse themselves in their work to the extent where their health and private life starts to suffer. As Priest and Gass (1997: p300) suggest:

> *...most of us have strong commitments to our work, serving in a very altruistic manner that requires us to give certain levels of self-sacrifice and service to others. Such a high level of commitment can produce a great deal of energy, empowerment, and positive results for clients, but can also prove expensive to us personally...we often pour so much effort into others that we neglect to take care of ourselves.*

The result of this combination of neglect and commitment can be burnout. This often manifests itself as physical, emotional and mental exhaustion that, if left untreated, can lead to very real illness and long-term debilitation. Unfortunately one of the few ways to address burnout once it has occurred is through long-term rest and a reduced workload after returning to the workplace. Not surprisingly this is something that many leaders, who feel a great deal of ownership for their work, are reluctant to contemplate. This naturally leads to a vicious downward spiral which if not stemmed can lead to total mental and physical collapse. Burnout, therefore, is very definitely one problem that is better prevented than treated.

Given the work often done by leaders working with young people (see section on emotions below) one of the keys to avoiding burnout is to have an understanding employer and strong support network. These allow you to 'offload' some of your problems by talking them through and looking at alternative strategies. It is also vital, and indeed obvious, that overloading with work is avoided and that you feel confident enough to say when you have reached your limits. Following on from this it is important to recognise the very early signs of burnout which may include feelings of hopelessness, incompetence and low self-esteem, nagging or constant tiredness for no obvious reason, irritability, finding excuses to avoid work and difficulties with concentration. It takes courage to admit to the early signs of burnout but it needs to be emphasised that burnout is not an inability to cope; it is very often the opposite and is more akin to coping with too much. Burnout at this stage should not be neglected but discussed with your employers or colleagues and a strategy put forward, which will almost certainly involve some time spent away from work to put things back into perspective.

One very significant problem is that as leaders working with young people we tend to have high expectations, high hopes and aspirations as well as high values and standards. It is when others do not meet these high ideals that leaders can really start to suffer from burnout, especially if there is a lack of congruence between the ideals of the leader and the leader's employers. It is even worse when the leader themselves fails to live up to the standards, maybe impossible standards, that they aspire to live by. Realism, as mentioned elsewhere (see Chapter 13 Measuring Success) is therefore a key factor in avoiding burnout, although finding an employer with the same ethos as yourself is perhaps even better: providing you don't both end up with burnout!

Another key determinant in burnout is not setting clear boundaries with the young people in your charge. Although it may be important to allow young people to have access to you in your own time for emergencies or crises this should not be allowed to get out of hand. Some leaders happily give their phone numbers to anyone with instructions to call them whenever needed whilst others maintain a strict boundary between work time and own time. Obviously a lot will depend on the nature of the work you are doing but if you do need to allow access at non-work times clear boundaries and criteria should be set.

Finally, it is always worth noting:

> *...when you are up to your backside in crocodiles and bugs,*
> *it can be hard to remember that*
> *your original intention was to admire the marsh flowers.*

One way to stave off burnout, if not to avoid it, is to remember what it was that inspired you to work as a leader with young people, take a break, recharge your batteries, revisit your vision (Chapter 2) and come back to your original motivation and purpose. Remove the cause of the long-term stress by replacing it with short-term challenges, of your choice and under your control, relate these to your original vision and concentrate on them.

Coping with Emotions

It is easier said than done but if we never left work behind the emotions involved would simply pile up and eventually swamp us. If you are dealing with issues such as abuse or dependency where strong emotions are aroused you need to consider how you are going to handle those feelings.

The first, and most important, rule is to be honest with yourself and others. There is no point helping someone else offload their problems if they are simply transferred to you and then you find yourself going under. All workers who deal with strong emotions need someone to talk to, ideally in a professional capacity. This can, however, come from outside of the work environment as well as from within.

In Chapter 4 we spoke of the importance of leaders, but especially leaders working with young people, being able to compartmentalise their feelings and emotions so that one situation doesn't spill out into another. This obviously has one major disadvantage for the leader concerned. Imagine that you have had a blazing row with a colleague, you have then had to go straight into working with the young people in your charge so, as a responsible leader should, you have pushed those feelings and anger to the back of your mind. At the end of a long evening you leave the youth club where you are working feeling tired and drained, but that anger and raw emotion is still there gnawing away, so you have a bad night's sleep. The following morning you are tired, irritable and still dwelling on the anger, but now you have to push it back again so that you can do your work. It is easy to see how a vicious downward spiral has started to take control. Compartmentalising emotions doesn't mean simply locking emotions away; they will emerge eventually. The aim of dealing with emotions in this way is to allow them to be expressed or dealt with at an appropriate time and place, preferably of your choosing.

Whilst it is important that you separate your own feelings and emotions from your work with young people it is also important that you look after yourself. We all have different ways of coping with such situations, some will have regular counselling or confide in friends and family while others may take up sport; 'to blow off steam'. The important thing is that the feelings and emotions are dealt with in a positive manner rather than being left to wreak emotional havoc at a later date. Incidentally, although a leader should never take out their emotions on the young people they work with, it is important that we are honest with them; there is usually nothing wrong with saying something like 'look, I've had a lousy day and I'm feeling really wound up, but it's nothing to do with you guys so just ignore me if I seem ratty tonight'. Young people may often seem as if they only care about themselves and are insensitive to the moods of others but this is usually a façade put on in order to appear 'cool' and they can be surprisingly understanding and non-judgemental.

Chapter 13

Measuring Success

O wad some power the giftie gie us to see ourselves as others see us.　　(Robert Burns)

Although it can be very intangible and difficult to gauge, it is important to have some idea of the success, or otherwise, of your role as a leader. Wheal (1998: p164) points out that:

In all work with young people it is important to evaluate what you are doing, why was it done that way, was there a better way?...it is important to stand back to evaluate in order to avoid complacency or missing important pointers.

Chapter 2 (Developing a unique way of working) discussed how experience is an important component of a leader's make-up and way of working and highlighted that this experience had to be evaluated and developed in a constructive way. As Paul Petzoldt (cited in Graham, 1997: p18) says:

There are too many people with a lot of experience who don't know what they're doing...I know people who've been making the same mistakes for years.

Experiential learning as a tool is often wrongly considered to be purely a matter of learning from experience, it is however much more than this. To truly benefit from any learning experience it has to be put into context and analysed and this is even more important when learning from experience. Experience by itself is simply an experience gained, it is only when all the lessons have been drawn from the experience that it can be considered to be experiential learning (Dewey, 1938). As Teschner and Wolter (1990: p280) say:

Even high quality experiences do not result in learning unless complemented by equally high quality reflection.

In this chapter, however, we are concerned with more than the learning experienced by the leader working with young people, we are also concerned with the learning engaged in by young people and how to measure the success, or otherwise, of what has been achieved. We are therefore looking to do several things:

- Develop and utilise the learning engendered by the leader's experience.
- Develop and encourage the learning engendered by the experience of the young people.
- Gauge the effectiveness of the learning and development undertaken by the young people.
- Gauge the effectiveness of the work done by the leader.
- Look forward to any improvements that can be made in any of these areas.

The key to all these areas is fortunately very similar and revolves around the idea of evaluation. It is important that evaluation is seen as an extension of reviewing which was covered in Chapter 9 Reviewing and Feedback.

Evaluation

It needs to be highlighted from the start that although evaluation and reviewing are similar, and may use very similar techniques, they are not the same. Greenaway (1993: p15) highlights the differences as:

The main purpose of reviewing is to increase value: the main purpose of evaluation is to judge value.

Or in other words; reviewing is helping people to learn whilst evaluation is finding out what people have learnt. There is often a degree of confusion with terminology with reviewing and evaluation; a good example being the 'end of course review' where lessons are learnt for future courses. This is usually an evaluative process rather than a reviewing process. It is important, if not vital, that the distinction is borne in mind. This section concerns itself with evaluation as both a way of measuring success, or otherwise, and how to build on that success. Conversely, of course, evaluation can also be used to see where a programme or leader is going wrong and help put a mechanism into place to improve on what is happening. It is important to stress that evaluation does not only have to take place at the end of an exercise or programme, it can also be built in to allow for modification or adaptations to be made.

It is important when approaching an evaluation exercise that it is clear what needs to be evaluated. In many ways the difficulty in answering this question reflects the difficulty in gauging what is success when working with young people (see section below). It is important, however, to not only have an idea of what needs to be evaluated but also who will be seeing the results, these two factors will influence the type of evaluation undertaken. There are essentially three approaches to evaluation (Greenaway, 1996: p42):

1. A standardised approach that allows comparisons between programmes.
2. A tailor-made approach which is specific to a particular programme.
3. An open-ended, creative approach that may pick up more insightful suggestions that more systematic approaches might miss.

Obviously each approach to evaluation has its pros and cons. Funding bodies might prefer the standardised approach because it allows a direct comparison of effectiveness between programmes (see discussion below) but it could miss significant issues unique to that programme. The tailor-made approach can be fitted to specific questions and issues which the leader, or other evaluator, is concerned about but only make sense to people who were actually involved with the programme. Finally the open-ended approach may well fit in with the philosophy of a programme and avoid a 'jarring' return to reality but it could also avoid any real issues which people are reluctant to bring up. In reality many evaluations will use a combination of all three approaches with a few 'standard' questions, a few 'tailor-made' questions and an open discussion or 'any other comments' section. The question needs to be asked, however, if this attempt at keeping everyone happy is finally satisfying no one. Evaluation, which tries to be all things to all people, is of necessity a lengthy process and will in all likelihood be inappropriate at the end of a course or programme. The decision needs to be made, therefore, as to what is the final objective of the evaluation being carried out.

It is important, however, when evaluating work with young people that there is some sort of systematic approach: a simple 'did the programme work for you?' will not get any worthwhile response. Likewise it is also a necessity to separate out what was the objective of the programme. For example, if the programme revolved around a series of activities, which were designed to encourage teamwork, and the young people were asked 'which was the best activity?' they would probably suggest the activity that was the most fun. This, obviously, doesn't answer the question which most concerns the programme.

To develop a more useful form of evaluation in the example above it would be more beneficial to:

- List the activities.
- Have a score out of ten for each one for fun.
- Have a score out of ten for each one for learning about teamwork.
- Have a comment asking what was the best feature for each activity.

- Have a comment asking what was the worse feature for each activity.
- Have the same for overall scores and comments.
- Have the same for other features of the programme, including the leadership.

It would be best when working with younger children to turn this into a fun activity in its own right using 'chuff charts', physical activity or drawings (see Chapter 9 Reviewing and Feedback). Usually the most constructive way of running an evaluation session would be to hand out sheets with the comments above, or something similar, give time for personal reflection and writing and then finish with a group discussion to draw out similarities. It could also be an interesting activity to ask the young people to redesign the day, or programme, as they would have done it. Incidentally, simply giving out evaluation sheets and asking to have them returned at a later date never, ever, works.

What is Success?

Success, when applied to leadership with young people is an almost indefinable quantity: and yet we are so often asked to quantify what we do in terms of success or failure (or worse, in terms of cost effectiveness). Take the following example, a true story:

A project was designed and developed to take young people off the street from an inner-city environment, give them a basic training in leadership skills, and then use them as assistant leaders with other young people so that, over time, the project would become self-sustaining. However, the project team quickly found that once the young people had been removed from where they were squatting, given a bit of motivation and interest as well as a few skills they were finding jobs and leaving the project. This meant that the project constantly struggled to find young people as helpers and the project team were never getting beyond the initial stage of recruiting and training. As the objective of the project was for it to be led by young people trained by the project team this result was deemed, by whoever was holding the purse strings, to be unsuccessful and the project was closed down.

Success in the work of a leader with young people is often (probably too often) defined by outside and unrealistic criteria. In the example above the difficulty was that once the young people became employed they lost their funding; but could a project that had successfully taken a number of young people out of squats, solvent addiction and criminal lifestyles, given them motivation, basic skills and found them jobs truly be a failure simply because it had not fulfilled the initial brief? To return to a quote found at the very start (Chapter 2 Vision and Styles) of this book:

> When I was a newly qualified teacher I was seriously expecting a glamorous life, filled with moments of learning breakthroughs and touching pastoral Dead Poet's Society hugs and personal revelations. It took me about three months to realise that this was total garbage, and if I wanted my working life to mean anything it would be because Darren actually remembered his homework diary after two weeks of persuasion.   (Warren, 2001: p48)

Success, in this instance, was not about exam results or league tables it was about the small victory of a single young person doing something as simple as remembering a homework dairy. Not something that could realistically be put into an end of year report; but a success none the less. One major difficulty is that the whole field of leadership with young people tends to be defined in cliché or glib terms. For example, we happily talk about a programme fostering 'personal development or growth' but does this mean intellectual growth, a growth in independence, technical growth, psychological growth, maturity, or all of these or something else entirely. Whilst these are questions for the field as a whole to answer it is also important that individual leaders make some attempt to rationalise what they are trying to achieve.

There are, however, occasional moments when success, although intangible in financial or quantifiable terms is very real. These momentary experiences can be explained by the concepts of peak experiences or, as they are more usually known, 'magic moments'.

Magic moments

Many people working with or leading young people find that their work is a series of magic moments with sometimes long periods of routine in between. These moments, which are more than just moments of positive feedback, are renowned as giving what can be a difficult job its meaning and value. Magic moments can be great 'milestone' moments such as completing an important project or winning a tournament but they are much more likely to arise in the period building up to the climax when everything seems to be coming together. It is also quite likely that magic moments can arise over something as simple as sharing a meal or tea break with a group of young people. Technically magic moments can be divided into three groups:

Flow

This is a physical state bought about through activity at an optimum level in terms of physical and mental ability. This tends to be a very individual feeling where external stimuli are reduced to a minimum. Sports people often refer to flow as 'being in the groove' but it can also be seen at its most powerful when top chess players become totally emerged in a game.

Peak experiences

These tend to have more spiritual and emotional connotations than flow. They are often exemplified by feelings of 'quietness' and 'being at one' with nature or a deity or sharing with other people. Some people speak of peak experiences as 'transcendence'.

Plateau experiences

These are the experiences most commonly referred to as magic moments. They are of a lesser intensity than peak experiences and refer to moments of shared experiences and a feeling of calmness or 'togetherness'.

Maslow (1964: p62) who did much of the original work on magic moments, in particular peak experiences, wrote that:

> *...so many people find [peak experiences] so great and high an experience that it justifies not only itself but even living itself. Peak experiences can make living worthwhile by their occasional occurrence. They give meaning to life itself. They prove it to be worthwhile.*

It is important to note that Maslow saw peak experiences as essentially spiritual in nature, although not necessarily in terms of an organised religion. He goes so far as to define peak experiences as a 'rebirth' and in this context it is easy to see how these moments can be crucial to personal and group development.

The importance of these powerful momentary experiences is that people will not only remember them for a long time but they can also be moments when all the lessons and experiences of an experience or programme 'come together' and make sense. A leader cannot force these moments onto students, but by providing the right activities and experiences at the right level and at the right time they can provide the right circumstances for them to happen in.

Chapter 14

Rules, Roles and Responsibilities

This might seem like an odd chapter to place near the end of a book, one that many people might have put earlier. Here, however, it acts as a brief summary and finishing point as well as an aide-mémoire of some of the things discussed elsewhere.

Some Leadership Rules

There are some simple 'rules' of leadership that are always worth bearing in mind for anyone leading young people (see Chapter 12 for a discussion on the ethics of rules). These are:

A leader needs to be fair and must never be seen to be biased

This should go without saying but it can be difficult if some of the group you are working with are pleasant and easy to get on with and others are difficult. A leader should be careful how they distribute tasks and responsibilities; or even how much time they spend talking to certain people (Chapter 12 Allegations of abuse).

Leadership is not about ego

It cannot be denied that leadership, especially leadership with young people, acts as a major ego boost. This is particularly the case with younger leaders. A sensible leader will not deny this fact but be aware of it and question the way they act (Chapter 2 Vision and Styles).

Good leadership is often the ability to delegate effectively…however, ultimate responsibility can never be delegated

These are perhaps the most important points that the leader, must remember. It may be that they are working on building up levels of leadership or teamwork amongst a group of young people and in order to do this have handed over the running of the group to the group members. In order to delegate authority it is important that the leader has established themselves as the responsible leader of the group before handing over the running of the group (Chapter 2 Leadership styles). The leader does, of course, remain responsible for the actions, and well-being of the group, particularly so if they are under eighteen.

Often a student leader jumps in with the 'follow me, this is how we will do it' technique. One of the hard rules of leadership is that others may have better ideas that need to be both listened to and encouraged. A good leader is exemplified by the ability to encourage and use other people's skills and ideas. The blame, however, cannot be passed down if those skills and ideas fail to work.

A leader's behaviour towards members of the opposite sex must not be capable of being misconstrued

This should, hopefully, go without saying but it is very easy to fall into certain traps. For example, if teaching skills a leader must be careful not to always use a group member of the opposite sex to demonstrate on. A leader's behaviour must be beyond reproach; often even the most innocent of actions can be misconstrued and at best undermine their leadership or at worst get them into very real trouble (Chapter 12 Allegations of abuse and how to avoid them).

Criteria and standards set by the leader must be made clear from the start

A leader can't make up the rules as they go along. The standards must be set at the start and stuck to. This is particularly important when it comes to safety matters and the delegation of leadership (Chapter 2 Leadership styles).

Leaders must not be critical of others without very good reason and rarely, if ever, in public

If a leader is harsh towards a member of a group in public the other group members will usually quickly 'gang up' in support of them. If there is a need to criticise somebody they should be taken to one side.

A leader should also be very aware of the danger of discussing or criticising young people without their knowledge to fellow group members. This can easily be taken as 'backstabbing'.

The art of giving feedback is one that needs to be learnt and should usually take place in a controlled environment. It is perhaps wise not to allow young people to be too critical of each other, at least not in the early stages of their relationship (Chapter 9 Reviewing and Feedback).

The leader sets an example

It can be hard, but in front of a group of young people the leader must live by their own rules. Students are very quick to notice if they are in the river getting soaked and the leader is on the bank telling them that it won't hurt, likewise the leader can't always delegate the washing up! (Chapter 2 Leadership styles). It is also important to consider how the actions of a leader influence the actions of the young people in his charge. As Cooper (1998: p123) says:

> Young people are perceptive to the leader's actions...the leader who professes to be interested in empowering young people but who talks too much and continually interferes in their learning will also be obvious. The 'media', the actions of the leader, must match the message...A leader picking up litter from a foreshore and putting it in their bag without comment may provoke questions from individuals and provide a much stronger message than any amount of talking about litter collection.

And finally: a leader learns the names of the group!

Not only does this make for a more pleasant time but in a moment of crisis it may make all the difference between being understood or being ignored.

A group will never develop in either leadership or team spirit if they do not know each other's names. There are a whole variety of games that can be used to foster this (Chapter 6 Team building and bonding).

In addition to these, Wheal (1998: p3) quotes the code of ethics produced by the FICE (Fédération Internationale des Communicatives Éducatives) as being worthy of particular consideration. The code consists of the following clauses:

It is the professional responsibility of everyone to:

- *Value and respect a young person as an individual in their own right, in their role as a member of their family and in their role as a member of the community in which they live.*

- *Respect the relationship of the young person to their parents, their siblings and other members of their family, taking account of their natural ties and interdependent rights and responsibilities.*

- *Enable the normal growth and development of each individual young person to achieve their potential in all aspects of functioning.*

- *Help each young person for whom they have responsibility by preventing problems where possible, by offering protection where necessary, or by providing care and rehabilitation to counteract or resolve problems faced.*

- *Use information appropriately, respecting the privacy of young people, maintaining confidentiality where necessary and avoiding the misuse of personal information.*

- *Oppose at all time any form of discrimination, oppression or exploitation of young people and preserve their rights.*

- *Maintain personal and professional integrity, develop skills and knowledge in order to work with competence, work co-operatively with colleagues, monitor the quality of services, and contribute to the development of the service and of policy and thinking in the field.*

The Leader's Responsibilities

A leader not only takes responsibility for the young people in their charge but through that action also, automatically, assumes responsibility for many other things. Some of these responsibilities are shown in Figure 27 and listed below. An immediate observation, which this list, and experience, highlights is that many of these responsibilities are difficult to resolve and may even be contradictory. A book such as this cannot attempt to resolve such issues, only common sense, your conscience, experience and the advice of those more experienced than you can point a way through this seemingly unsolveable maze.

Many of these responsibilities are self-evident and few leaders will need reminding of them. Because of their importance however, and at the acknowledged risk of patronising people, they are presented here in some detail.

Relatives and parents

The close relatives of the young people a leader will be working with are very interested in their qualities as a leader because they are handing their relative's into their care. Obviously with the first responsibility of a leader being to the young people in their care there may be conflict, particularly with regard to confidentially, with parents and this responsibility can be a fine line which needs careful handling (Chapter 12 Allegations of abuse).

Yourself

This responsibility has been covered in some depth in Chapter 12 and does not need reiteration here except to say that you cannot meet any of your other responsibilities if you neglect this one!

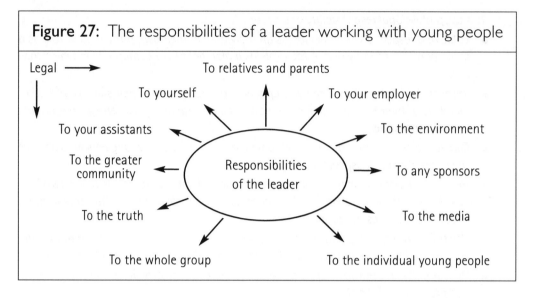

Figure 27: The responsibilities of a leader working with young people

Legal ⟶

To relatives and parents

To yourself

To your employer

To your assistants

To the environment

To the greater community

Responsibilities of the leader

To any sponsors

To the truth

To the media

To the whole group

To the individual young people

The media

Sadly it is unlikely that many leaders working with young people will come across the national media in a beneficial way, if they do come into contact with them it will often be because there has been an accident or incident of some sort. A leader should always attempt to be polite to reporters but **never** give the names of any young people involved in any incident. It is, however, always worth cultivating a friendly local paper that will be happy to run positive stories for you. Media coverage will aid you considerably, not only in terms of raising the profile and image of the young people you work with but also when it comes to getting support, and sponsorship, from others.

Sponsors

It may be that you will need to attract sponsors in order to carry out your work. If you are fortunate enough to be successful in this it does place you under an obligation, which can be demanding, to meet their needs, usually in terms of media coverage, public events, reporting back or photo displays.

The environment

All leaders have some responsibility to the environment in which they work and this need not necessarily be an outdoor environment. There has been a trend amongst a lot of educators in recent years to think globally but perhaps to neglect to act locally. Although the major international issues are, of course, important it is also important that leaders working with young people think about how they interact with their local environment and how things could be improved on a smaller, more immediate level.

Your employer

Whilst working with young people a leader is not only an advertisement for themselves but also for their employer. Likewise complaining about an employer to a group is unprofessional and unacceptable. In some cases it may be that the young people you work with have some sort of dispute with your employer, for example; they may be a youth group campaigning for better facilities against the council that employees you. There is no black and white solution to such a situation, it might be that you take a middle road by advising the young people on their best course of action but telling them you cannot be a part of it. Your conscience, and the nature of your employer, will have to be your guide (see Chapter 12 for a discussion on principle and value ethics which might influence this).

The truth

If you have succeeded in building a good bond with the young people that you work with there will be a high element of trust involved. This will often come down to sharing, communicating and being truthful (Chapter 4) with each other. You cannot expect to maintain the trust of those you work with unless you are truthful with them. It has been said that in conflict truth is the first victim; you may need to struggle to avoid such a situation.

The greater community

There was a time when leaders of young people were seen as acting for the good of the greater community rather than for the good of the young people involved. Things, thankfully, have now changed; however you should never lose sight of the wider implications of your actions.

Individual young people

This can be the hardest of all the responsibilities, a group is made up of individuals: a fact which is sometimes easy to overlook! The group as a whole may be working well together and having a great time but if one person is failing is the leader failing? Is the larger responsibility to the greater good or to the needier individual? (Chapter 3 Action centred leadership). There is no right or wrong solution to a situation like this: again it is all a clever balancing act.

Your assistants

It may sound strange that the leader could be responsible for any assistants that they might have. Obviously this will depend on the relationship between the leader and the assistants and their relative skills, qualifications and experience. It may well be, however, that the leader is not only responsible for the assistant's well-being but for their actions as well.

The whole group

To a large extent a leader's main responsibility is to the group of young people that they are working with. This may sound so obvious that it hardly needs saying but in many ways, as with individual young people, it can be the easiest of responsibilities to neglect. All of the responsibilities above need to be addressed and it may be that, as a leader, you are under considerable pressure from 'official' sources to meet them; the one responsibility that isn't nagging to be noticed might well be the group of young people that you would claim to be looking out for. This can be a difficult juggling act but it is always worth returning to your vision (Chapter 2) and reaffirming to yourself why is it that you are working as a leader with young people: this should usually resolve the conflicting demands.

Overall legal responsibilities

The responsibilities above are all encased in a box entitled 'legal'. The question of how much leaders working with young people should rigidly enforce the law is a difficult and contentious one, as already discussed in the responsibility to the greater community above (and in Chapter 12). However, moral and ethical issues aside it is the case that anyone working with young people is faced with an ever-increasing amount of legal responsibilities and legislation. This should not in any way put anyone off being a leader; most leaders will find that they can fulfil their responsibilities with a little common sense and without too much difficulty. The notable legal points to be aware of include:

In loco parentis

'In loco parentis' means quite simply 'in place of the parent', it implies that any person who has charge of young people, usually taken as under sixteen, sometimes as under eighteen, has the same duty of care for them as a responsible parent would have. This duty of care was defined in the 1989 Children Act as meaning that a person who has care of a child should do all that is reasonable, under the circumstances, for the purposes of safeguarding or promoting the welfare of the child. This is a serious and major responsibility for any leader as it may mean that they have total care, and must accept total responsibility, for any young people they work with. In practice the law works on the understanding of what could reasonably be foreseen. This means that if a leader has taken all practicable steps to ensure a young person's welfare in any reasonably foreseeable event they will be deemed to have carried out their duty. It is important to remember, however, that the law expects children to act in unpredictable ways and that a leader also needs to take this into account.

Unfortunately, it is not always clear who has the responsibility of 'in loco parentis', but it is safest to assume that, unless it has been formally handed over, the leader who took the young people out of the care of their parents or guardians has responsibility. This means, for example, that if a leader is taking a group of youngsters to a football coaching session and they are not happy with the coach running the session it is their responsibility to act. Many residential centres have a formal handing over of responsibility at the start and end of activity sessions to emphasise who is responsible at that time. This does not, however, entirely negate the 'in loco parentis' responsibility of the group leader; it simply infers that they have handed over to a person who is more expert in an activity than they are.

Duty of care

Whether there is a legal contract or not, any leader can be said to have a duty of care for the members of their group. This need not be an organised group in the commercial sense, if a leader sets themselves up as an expert in the eyes of a group they assume the responsibility that goes with it. This can even, theoretically, apply to a more experienced person taking part in an activity with a group of lesser experienced friends.

Activity Centres (Young Persons' Safety) Act 1995, see Chapter 11 The question of risk.

Minibus driving

Whilst not strictly always part of being a leader, many leaders who work with young people will have to drive a minibus at some time and should be aware of the minibus regulations. These can be complex but, in general, state that anyone driving a vehicle of more than eight seats, which has not been registered for educational or charitable purposes, needs the appropriate license or permit and, most importantly, the driver is responsible. There will also usually be local regulations to be met where local authority minibuses are to be used. It is always worth considering taking the full D1 driving course if you are going to be involved in driving minibuses, you cannot drive in Europe without one in any case. The minibus regulations seem to be in a constant state of flux and it is important to try to keep up with what is happening.

The Role of the Ideal Leader

Andrews (1997: p15) suggests that the roles of the ideal leader include:
   1. Defining the task—what it is and why you need to do it.
   2. Planning—co-ordinate and check effectiveness.
   3. Briefing—ensuring clear understanding of plan.
   4. Controlling—dealing with issues, keeping focused.
   5. Supporting—motivating and encouraging individuals.
   6. Informing—keeping everyone in the picture and linking.
   7. Monitoring—checking on progress.
   8. Reviewing—relating success rate, feedback and appraisal.

It can be clearly seen that this checklist is not only task oriented but also tends towards the autocratic leadership role identified in Chapter 2 and, as such, does little to engage the group in question. It does however, serve as a starting point for a summary of what a leader with young people does and is trying to achieve.

1. Defining the task

Action centred leadership demonstrates how the task is but one of three aspects to effective leadership and the role of the leader may be to develop the individual or group elements of the ACL model. The task may well be merely a guise under which other learning, empowerment or development takes place. However it may also be the primary focus of the exercise. In either case the motivation, nature, abilities, stage of team development and role of the young people involved, notably with regard to their responsibility and authority, needs to be considered.

2. Planning

The leader needs to identify the most appropriate leadership style, possibly through the use of the situational leadership model, in order to facilitate the planning stage of a task. This will, inevitably, come back to the purpose of the exercise or task as outlined above. Does the task, or the nature of the group, warrant the maximum input from the leader or can or should the planning be left to the young people involved? Does the task require that the leader ensures that the planning and decision making process is understood and followed or can the group be left to make their own mistakes and learn from them? The leader also needs to consider what areas of responsibility need to be addressed, particularly with regard to the effect of the task on outside agencies and other interested parties.

3. Briefing

Communication has been highlighted as one of the most important skills of a leader and nowhere is this more evident than in the briefing stage. The ability to convey information and to ensure that everyone is involved to the maximum of their abilities and interests is paramount. The significance of two-way communication will be apparent in this role. Whilst the anticipated learning outcomes of a task need not be overt there should be a clear purpose and aim.

4. Controlling

As with planning, the question here is how much should the leader intervene; reference to leadership styles will show that this need not be a fixed quantity but can vary as appropriate to the situation. Motivation is also important with the leader needing to ensure that the group remains on track or at least is given the understanding to appreciate why things are going adrift. Health and safety will need to be monitored by the leader, whatever the nature of the task, as will the appropriate behaviour and actions of the group.

5. Supporting

If leadership has largely been handed over to the young people involved then this may be the most significant role for the leader during the lifetime of the task itself. A positive display of caring leadership will encourage young people to have confidence in the leader's support and thereby the confidence needed to take risks in both the physical and emotional arenas. It is quite likely that this role will need focusing on both the group and individual dimensions in order for the task to be completed successfully. The leader needs to consider that different groups, or groups at different stages of development, will need, and want, different levels of support and act appropriately.

6. Informing

Communication, again, is vital if everybody involved is to feel committed to the task and aware of what is happening. It may be that the leader's informing role is supportive in that they are encouraging communication at the appropriate level amongst the group members rather than directly instigating communication. Appropriate feedback may be necessary in this role as will considering how motivation is being affected by information flow.

7. Monitoring

Whilst this role will involve a level of evaluation to ensure that the task or exercise is on track it will also be about providing the opportunities for reviewing the problem solving process and the participation and roles of the young people involved. Rather than being purely evaluative the leader needs to ensure that this element makes a significant and ongoing contribution to the learning process. It is possible that the leader may need to reconsider their role and orientation or the nature of the task to ensure that individuals and the group are maximising their learning potential. Likewise the leader may have to step in to maintain group cohesion or remove barriers to team development. This will usually depend on all those issues considered at the task defining and planning stages.

8. Reviewing

Andrew's model gives this element a largely evaluative role. Whilst this may be appropriate in a purely task-related environment it will rarely be so in a leadership with young people situation. Evaluation will be important for the task as well as internal and external performance evaluation and justification, but feedback and reviewing are likely to be much more pertinent to the leader's role. As in all experiential learning situations it is the quality of reviewing that will bring out the full potential of the learning environment. The success of the task will, in all likelihood, be approached first from the standpoint of the young people concerned and, secondly, from the viewpoint of other interested parties.

And Finally

Geoff Cooper (1998: p36) quotes Lao-Tse's definition of a good leader as being:

> *A leader is best when people barely know he exists, not so good when people obey and acclaim him, worst when they despise him...But of a good leader when his work is done, his aim fulfilled, they will say 'we did this for ourselves'.*

As an expression of a good leader working with young people this seems particularly apt. This book has discussed many facets of leadership, styles, roles, vision communication and so on. It has also consistently returned to the theme that leadership of young people is about facilitation, about helping young people to learn for themselves; to find their own answers.

This is hard for a leader who puts their heart and soul into a group of young people only to have to step back and let them take over and move on by themselves. Perhaps it is one reason why so many of the really good leaders of young people are unsung heroes: precisely because they have been able to let the young people in their charge say 'we did this by ourselves'.

References

Adair, J. (1988a). *The Action-centred Leader.* London: The Industrial Society.

Adair, J. (1988b). *Effective Leadership.* London: Pan Books Ltd.

Adair, J. (1990). *Understanding Motivation.* Guildford: Talbot Adair Press.

Allison, P. (2000). *Research from the Ground Up: Post-expedition Adjustment.* Ambleside: Brathay Hall Trust.

Andrews, R. (1997). *Adventure in Education.* Plymouth: Nortcote House Publishers.

Appleyard, B. (2001). It's So Unfair. *The Sunday Times*; Focus 5/8/01: p16.

Baker-Graham, A. (1999). Working with Girls and Young Women. In Higgins, P., and Humberstone, B. (Eds.) (1999). *Outdoor Education and Experiential Learning in the UK.* Luneburg: Zeitschrift fur Erlebnispadagogik.

Barnes, P. (1997). An Introduction to the Study of Staff Motivation. *Horizons*, 14(3): pp3–6.

Barnes, P. (Ed.) (2000). *Values and Outdoor Learning.* Penrith: AfOL Publications.

Bass, B. (1989). *Stogdill's Handbook of Leadership: A Survey of Theory and Research.* New York: Free Press.

Belbin, M. (1983). *Management Teams: Why They Succeed or Fail.* Oxford: Butterworth Heinemann.

B.T. (1997). *Talkworks.*

Cooper, G. (1998). *Outdoors with Young People.* Lyme Regis: Russell House Publishing.

Davies, B. (1986). *Threatening Youth.* Milton Keynes: Open University Press.

Dewey, J. (1916). *Democracy and Education.* New York: The Free Press.

Dewey, J. (1938). *Experience and Education.* New York: Collier Books.

Dodd, C. (1990). *Conversations with Mothers and Daughters.* London: Optima.

Factor, F., Chauhan, V., and Pitts, J. (Eds.) (2001). *The RHP Companion to Working with Young People.* Lyme Regis: Russell House Publishing.

Fox, R. (2000). Enhancing Spiritual Experience in Adventure Programs. In Miles, J.C., and Priest, S. (Eds.) *Adventure Programming.* State College, Pennsylvania: Venture Publishing Inc., pp455–461.

Gass, M.A. (1985). Programming the Transfer of Learning in Adventure Education. In Kraft, R., and Sakofs, M. (Eds.) *The Theory of Experiential Education*, pp131–142. Boulder: The Association for Experiential Education.

Graham, J. (1997). *Outdoor Leadership.* Seattle: The Mountaineers.

Greenaway, R. (1993). *Playback.* Windsor: The Duke of Edinburgh's Award.

Greenaway, R. (1996). *Reviewing Adventures, Why and How.* Sheffield: NAOE Publications.

Handy, C. (1993). *Understanding Organisations.* London: Penquin.

Henderson, K. (1999). Should Gender-specific Programs, Such as All Women Courses be Offered in Adventure Education? Yes Perspective. In Wurdinger and Potter (1999) (op cit).

Hersey, P., and Blanchard, K. (1982). *Management of Organizational Behaviour: Utilizing Human Resources* (4th edn). Englewood Cliffs, NJ: Prentice-Hall.

Hopkins, D., and Putnam, R. (1993). *Personal Growth Through Adventure.* London: David Fulton Publishers.

Humberstone, B. (1984). Learning for a Change: A Study of Schooling in Outdoor Education. In Evans, J. (Ed.). *PE, Sport and Schooling, Studies in the Sociology of PE.* Lewis: Falmer Press.

Jeffs, T., and Smith, M. (1998). The Problem of 'Youth' for youth work. *Youth and Policy*, 62: pp45–66.

Jones, J.E. (1973). A model of Group Development. In Jones, J.E., and Pfeiffer, J.W. *The Annual Handbook for Group Facilitators.*

King, C.K. (1985). *The Words of Martin Luther King.* London: Fount Paperbacks.

Kolb, D. (1984). *Experiential Learning.* Englewood Cliffs, NJ: Prentice-Hall.

Lawlor, M., and Handley, P. (1996). *The Creative Trainer: Holistic Facilitation Skills for Accelerated Learning.* London: McGraw-Hill.

Luft, J. (1961). The Johari Window. In Luthans, F. (1977). *Organisational Behaviour.* New York: Mcgraw-Hill.

Lynch, J. (1999). Should Gender-specific Programs, Such as All Women Courses be Offered in Adventure Education? No Perspective. In Wurdinger and Potter (1999) (op cit)

Maddern, E. (2000). Pathways to Manhood: Tackling the Problems of Boys Growing up. In Barnes (2000) (op cit), pp137–143.

Maslow, A. (1943). A Theory of Motivation. Cited in Adair (1990) (op cit).

Maslow, A. (1964). *Religions, Values and Peak Experiences.* New York: Penquin-Arkana.

Mason, V. (1995). *Sport in England.* London: Sports Council.

McClelland, D. (1961). The Achieving Society. Cited in Barnes (1997) (op cit).

McCormack, J., and Spratt, G. (1996). *Discovery Project Recordings* (unpublished).

Morrow, V., and Richards, M. (1996). *Transition to Adulthood.* York: Joseph Rowntree Foundation.

Mortlock, C. (1984). *The Adventure Alternative.* Milnthorpe: Cicerone Press.

Nolan, V. (1987). *Teamwork.*

Ogilvie, K. (1993). *Leading and Managing Groups in the Outdoors.* Sheffield: NAOE Publications.

Petri, H.L. (1991). *Motivation; Theory, Research and Applications.* California: Wadsworth Publishing.

Priest, S. (1990). Thoughts on Managing Dangers in Adventure Programmes. *Journal for Adventure Education and Outdoor Leadership*, 13(1).

Priest, S., and Gass, M. (1994). Frontloading with Paradox and Double Binds in Adventure Education Facilitation. *Journal of Adventure Education and Outdoor Leadership*, 11(1).

Priest, S., and Gass, M. (1997). *Effective Leadership in Adventure Programming.* Leeds: Human Kinetics.

Raven, B.H., and Rubin, J.E. (1975). *Social Psychology: People in Groups.* New York: John Wiley and Sons.

Rea, J., and Slavkin, M. (2000). The Gender Based Relationships of Girls to their Natural Environment. In Barnes (2000) (op cit), pp89–96.

Rose, G. (1993). *Feminism and Geography.* Oxford: Polity Press.

Scraton, S. (1986). Images of Femininity and the Teaching of Girls' PE. In Evans, J. (Ed.) *Ped, Sport and Schooling.* Lewis: Falmer Press.

Scraton, S. (1992). *Shaping up to Womanhood: Gender and Girls' Physical Education.* Buckinghamshire: Open University Press

Spence, J. (1990). Youth Work and Gender. In Jeffs, T., and Smith, M. (Eds.) *Young People, Inequality and Youth Work.* Buckingham: Open University Press.

Spratt, G., Khom, N., and Crowther, C (1998). *Youth and Social Work on the Move.* Vienna: University of Vienna.

Spratt, G., McCormack, J., and Collins, D. (1998). The Discover Project: A Perspective from the United Kingdom. In Higgins, P., and Humberstone, B. (Eds.) *Celebrating Diversity: Learning by Sharing Cultural Differences.* Buckinghamshire: EIOAEEL.

Squirrel, G. (1999). *Developing Social Skills.* Lyme Regis: Russell House Publishing.

Steers, R.M., and Porter, L.W. (1991). *Motivation and Work Behaviour.* New York: McGraw-Hill.

Sugarman, L. (1986). *Life-span Development: Concepts, Theories and Interventions.* London: Methuen.

Tannerbum, R., and Schimdt, W.H. (1973). How to Choose a Leadership Pattern. *Harvard Business Review*, 51(3): pp162–275/178–180.

Tayfor, S. (1995). *Law Cartoons.* Tort. London: Sweet and Maxwell.

Teschner, D.P., and Wolter, J.J. (1990). Beyond Minimum Competencies. In Miles, J.C., and Priest, S. (Eds.) *Adventure Education.* State College, PA: Venture Publishing Inc.

Thompson, S.M. (1990). Thank the Ladies for the Plates: The Incorporation of Women into Sport. *Leisure Studies*, 9(2): pp135–43.

Tuckerman, B.W., and Jensen, M.A. (1977). Stages of Small Group Development Revisited. *Group and Organisation Studies*, 2(4): pp419–427.

Warren, G. (2001). A bit of Road Rage is a Wonderful Thing. *The Times Education Supplement*, 3/8/01: p48.

Warren, K. (1996). Women's Outdoor Adventures: Myth and Reality. In Warren, K. (Ed.) *Women's Voices in Experiential Education.* Boulder, CO: Association for Experiential Education, pp10–17.

Webb, M. (2001). Black Young People. In Factor, Chauhan and Pitts (2001) (op cit).

Weiner, B.M. (1974). *Achievement Motivation and Attribution Theory.* New Jersey: General Learning Press.

Wharton (1996). Health and Safety in Outdoor Activity Centres. *Journal for Adventure Activities and Outdoor Leadership*, 12(4).

Wheal, A. (1998). *Adolescence: Positive Approaches for Working with Young People.* Lyme Regis: Russell House Publishing.

Wilson, L. (1995). When We Want to Empower as Well as Teach. In Warren et al. (Eds.) *The Theory of Experiential Education.* Dubuque, IA: Kendall Hunt Publishing Company, pp. 275–283.

Wubbolding, R.E., and Brickell, J. (1999). *Counselling with Reality Therapy.* Speechmark Publishing Ltd.

Wurdinger, S.D. (1997). *Philosophical Issues in Adventure Education* (3rd edn.). Dubuque, IA: Kendall Hunt Publishing Company.

Wurdinger, S.D., and Potter, T.G. (Eds.) (1999). *Controversial Issues in Adventure Education: A Critical Examination.* Dubuque, IA: Kendall Hunt Publishing Company.

Young, K. (1999). *The Art of Youth Work.* Lyme Regis: Russell House Publishing.